# Planning Facilities
# for Sci-Tech Libraries

# Planning Facilities for Sci-Tech Libraries

Ellis Mount, Editor

The Haworth Press
New York

*Planning Facilities for Sci-Tech Libraries* has also been published as *Science & Technology Libraries*, Volume 3, Number 4, Summer 1983.

The Haworth Press, Inc., 28 East 22 Street, New York, NY 10010

**Library of Congress Cataloging in Publication Data**
Main entry under title:

Planning facilities for sci-tech libraries.

"Has also been published as Science & technology libraries; volume 3, number 4, summer 1983."
Includes bibliographical references.
1. Technical libraries—Addresses, essays, lectures.
2. Scientific libraries—Addresses, essays, lectures.
3. Library planning—Addresses, essays, lectures.
4. Library architecture—Addresses, essays, lectures.
I. Mount, Ellis.
Z675.T3P53 1983        026'.5        83-8570
ISBN 0-86656-237-0

# Planning Facilities
# for Sci-Tech Libraries

Science & Technology Libraries
Volume 3, Number 4

## CONTENTS

EDITORIAL                                                              1

Guidelines for Planning Facilities for Sci-Tech Libraries             3
    *Howard Rovelstad*

Remodelled Library Facilities of the Oregon Regional
    Primate Research Center                                          21
    *Isabel G. McDonald*

Adapting Non-Library Facilities for Periodical Collections at
    Brookhaven National Laboratory                                  31
    *Ken Ryan*
    *Marilyn Galli*

Design of Library Facilities for the Ontario Ministry of
    Transportation and Communications                               43
    *Stefanie A. Pavlin*
    *Guna Plumanis*
    *Laila R. Zvejnieks*

Library Facilities for the Riley Stoker Corporation                 51
    *Cosette M. Kotseas*

Creating New Library Facilities for the Bendix Advanced
    Technology Center                                               59
    *Ted Rupprecht*

Facilities for Northwestern University's Science-Engineering
    Library                                                     77
                    *Janet Ayers*

Facilities of the Kresge Engineering Library at the
    University of California, Berkeley                          85
                    *Patricia Davitt Maughan*

Facilities of Swarthmore College's Science and Engineering
    Library                                                     95
                    *Michael J. Durkan*
                    *Emi K. Horikawa*

NEW REFERENCE WORKS IN SCIENCE AND
    TECHNOLOGY                                                 105
                    *Janice W. Bain, Editor*

SCI-TECH ONLINE                                                109
                    *Ellen Nagle, Editor*

SCI-TECH IN REVIEW                                             115
                    *Suzanne Fedunok, Editor*

# Planning Facilities
# for Sci-Tech Libraries

# EDITORIAL

Involvement in the planning of new or remodeled facilities for a library or information center, coupled with the processes of watching the plans being carried out and moving into completed facilities, can be both exhilarating and demanding. Librarians and information specialists who take part in such experiences find the rewards great in terms of a sense of creating a useful, attractive facility, but most people find they must pay for their accomplishments with a great deal of time and effort.

The purpose of this issue is to present some guidelines for those contemplating planning sci-tech library facilities, along with a number of reports on recent actual examples of such projects, representing a variety of sci-tech library types.

Those getting involved in library planning for the first time should profit from the initial article, a discussion of important guidelines for planning for sci-tech libraries. It is written by Howard Rovelstad, a consultant with many years of experience from which to draw upon.

Next follow examples from three libraries representing research libraries with strong government support or sponsorship. The first is by Isabel G. McDonald at the Oregon Regional Primate Research Center, who describes relocating the library into new quarters. Next is the description of the adapting of non-library facilities so as to accommodate periodicals for the Brookhaven National Laboratory, written by Ken Ryan and Marilyn Galli. Following this is an account of the creation of a new library for the Ontario Ministry of Transportation and Communications by Stefanie A. Pavlin, Guna Plumanis and Laila R. Zvejnieks.

Two corporate library facilities appear next, the first by Cosette M. Kotseas describing her library at the Riley Stoker Corporation. The other article is by Ted Rupprecht, who tells of the moving of most of one collection to another state for a new library for the Bendix Advanced Technology Center.

The remaining three papers concern university and college sci-tech libraries, beginning with Janet Ayers' account of the development of the science-engineering library at Northwestern University. Next is a description of the engineering library built for the University of California at Berkeley, written by Patricia Davitt Maughan. Then comes a report on Swarthmore College's science and engineering library, written by Michael J. Durkan and Emi K. Horikawa. Our regular features complete the issue.

*Ellis Mount, Editor*

# Guidelines for Planning Facilities for Sci-Tech Libraries

## Howard Rovelstad

**ABSTRACT.** A procedure is described for planning or for a major renovation of a science-technology library facility. Included are the preparation of the librarian for the task, the formation of a planning committee, selection of an architect, the possible use of a consultant, and the writing of a program statement with projections of space requirements for five years or more of collections, services and staff for the guidance of the architect.

## *INTRODUCTION*

Planning new library quarters or major renovations of library quarters for science and technology libraries includes a number of steps: First, the preparation of the librarian and management of the organization; next the development of a program statement including preliminary decisions on objectives, location, furnishings and financial limitations; and finally decisions on specifics of control and space requirements for services, materials and staff. These steps can be applied to small and large libraries, and to all kinds of libraries. Planning for a small library may require no more than several days while planning for a large one may require many months, but the procedure to be followed for each is the same. The possibility of a planning assignment early in a librarian's career should not be considered to be a remote possibility. Many librarians with few years of service have been given just such an assignment.

Defining what science and technology libraries are cannot be done easily and in a few words, since they are often part of a university or public library, or of a corporate organization. They

Howard Rovelstad has been a consultant on library buildings since 1960. He has been Director of Libraries Emeritus for the University of Maryland since 1975. His address is 11 Banbury Road, Gibson Island, MD 21056.

vary widely in size, functions and responsibilities. Because of this wide variance, guidelines in planning must necessarily be general in scope and only suggestive. Certainly not all of the procedures explained here will be applicable to all libraries. However, by following guidelines that seem applicable and by reading sources suggested in the bibliography and elsewhere, the librarian should be able to proceed in a logical and purposeful way to plan for a new library or for renovation of an existing library facility.

Although most of the literature on library planning has been written about public, school, college or university libraries, much of what has been said is applicable to science and technology libraries. Furthermore, many science libraries exist in public library systems and on university campuses. In addition, there are some works on planning special libraries, but comparatively little has been written about planning science and technology libraries specifically.

## INITIAL STEPS TO PREPARE THE WAY

It is assumed that the need for a new library or the renovation of a library has been justified on the basis of the economic advantage of the facility to the organization or on some other basis, and that management has approved the project.

At this time the librarian must prepare himself/herself, if he/she has not already done so, to provide the direction and leadership for those involved in the planning of the facility. Although it is usually the head librarian who acts in this capacity, in a large library another member of the professional staff, the deputy librarian for example, may assume the responsibility. This responsibility is critical as the librarian must not only gather information but also pass it on to management, to the library staff, to the advisory committee, and, most importantly, to the architect. In order to avoid surprises and to be assured that all parties in the building process agree with the final outcome, the librarian must keep everyone informed and must encourage criticism and suggestions. Changes can be made easily in the early stages of planning.

As the librarian involved in a building project often has not kept up with the literature on the subject, he/she must now survey what is available for use. As stated earlier, much information is available in journals and books in the library field and also some, in addition, in architectural publications. *Library Literature*[1] will provide references to most recent literature. Several books will be particularly helpful in providing basic information needed for a building project of any type of library. Keyes D. Metcalf's *Planning Academic and Research Library Buildings*[2] will serve as a comprehensive manual dealing with the whole range of planning and construction. The work, published in 1965, is currently being revised and up-dated by David C. Weber and Philip D. Leighton. The new edition will be published by the American Library Association (ALA) in 1984. Godfrey Thompson's *Planning and Design of Library Buildings*,[3] 2nd edition, published in 1977, also includes in its scope full planning and building processes. In *Mason On Library Buildings*[4] Ellsworth Mason devotes the first 60 pages to library building problems and then about 270 pages to reviewing and evaluating existing buildings, and to a model building program for a library. The Special Libraries Association (SLA), Monograph number 4, edited by Ellis Mount, *Planning the Special Library*,[5] has much helpful information for planners of science library facilities. Each of these books has much basic and essential information presented in such a way that the librarian can easily understand and apply it. They are also essential reading for the architect. The bibliography at the end of this article includes other books and also journal articles that seem particularly pertinent.

With this background the librarian should select a few libraries that operate somewhat in the same way as his/her own to visit. They should be carefully selected. Generally examples of good library planning are more helpful than examples of poor planning, but something can be learned of what not to do from the latter sites. Librarians who have worked in new quarters for a year or more may be able to give sound critical opinions about their facilities.

Suggestions of libraries to visit are available in the Mason book referred to above and in the annual summary of library building activities published in the December 1 issues of the *Library Journal*. In the December 1, 1981 issue, pages 2277-2286,[6] and in the December 1, 1982 issue, pages 2219-2220,[7] are brief, general statements of activities during 1981 and 1982 including academic and public library buildings, and also a list of the architects with their addresses who planned the buildings. In each category of libraries are included new libraries, additions and renovations. For each project reported information is given on cost, gross area assignable and non-assignable spaces, square foot costs, equipment costs, book and seating capacities and the architect. In the earlier issue two medical libraries, a law library and a polytechnic state university library are included, as well as others pertinent to special libraries.

The librarian can further prepare for the task ahead by attending conferences, institutes and seminars usually planned as preconference activities of annual meetings of library associations and, more recently, by attending seminars offered by commercial enterprises. Charles Finnerty recently taught an SLA continuing education course on library space planning. A preconference institute at the ALA Philadelphia 1982 conference entitled Building Libraries for Bibliographic Instruction and User Accessibility was given by the Buildings and Equipment Section of the Library Administration and Management Association. The Proceedings of this institute are now available on two cassettes (ALA 82/451-452) from the Order Department, ALA. The conference program on Theft in Libraries was also of much interest to library planners.

There is one other source to tap early in the preparation for planning—headquarters libraries or information managers of associations. The ALA Headquarters Library collection of programs, architectural plans, slides, etc. is available on loan. The library will supply a checklist of publications, many of which are useful for planning facilities. These are free or available at a nominal charge. The library has a special collection of building folders and slides, entries to the biennial competition for the best library building and renovation sponsored by the Library Administration and Management Association and the American Institute of Architects. Loans are made without charge except for postage to any library. Resources are sufficient to justify an on-site examination of them. Membership in ALA is not required.

Valuable information on library building standards is available for some types of libraries. ALA and its divisions have approved these standards: Guidelines for Branch Libraries in Colleges and Universities; Standards for College Libraries; Standards for University Libraries; and Guidelines for Two-Year College Learning Resources Programs. Marsha L. Selmer has prepared for the Committee on Standards, Geography and Map Division, SLA, Draft Standards for University Map Libraries.[8] These examples of standards include statements about physical plants. Although most of the standards are not written for science and technology libraries specifically, their coverage and general requirements may be useful. Other statements of standards may be more applicable to a local situation.

The theme of the Summer 1982 issue of *Library Trends*[9] is standards for library and information services, an issue concentrating "on service or performance standards as related to specific types of libraries." The section by James Beaupré Dodd, The Gap in Standards for Special Libraries,[10] relates the difficulties of establishing standards for special libraries and summarizes the activities in this field of SLA. Other sections deal with standards for state and health libraries, and for library services to people in institutions. There are many implications important to planning facilities for science libraries.

Early in the planning procedure consideration should be given to the appointment of an advisory planning committee, group or team composed of representatives of management of the parent organization, of potential users of the library, and perhaps members of the library staff in addition to the chief librarian, who in most situations would serve as chairman or leader. The size of the team would depend on the size and complexity of the building project. Full advantage should be taken of the expertise brought to the committee by its members, who must be informed of and given an opportunity to react to each major decision. Their opinions should be carefully weighed, but final authority on most library operations should rest with the librarian. By keeping the team well informed the organization will not be subject to surprises, and the librarian will be protected from any destructive criticism in the final outcome.

Sometime in early stages of planning a decision must be made concerning the possibility of employing a library building consultant to work with the librarian and team. The decision will be based on the size of the project, and the experience, expertise and time availability of the librarian. Although in the period after World War II until rather recent years some librarians had opportunities to be responsible for planning more than one building, many librarians have not experienced such an assignment and may, therefore, require the assistance of a consultant.

The consultant provides the experience and expertise lacking perhaps in the architect also. There are a few architects who have made a specialty of planning library facilities, and there should be an advantage in employing one of these, but most local architects lack this experience. A consultant also brings an outsider's opinion and influence, which may carry more persuasion than an insider's. Most always a consultant's fee will be paid for many times by his/her advice resulting in building cost economies and in an improved functional plan for the facility. The fees of a consultant are usually based on a per diem charge plus expenses, on a set fee or a percentage basis of the cost of the project. The amounts depend on the experience and reputation of the consultant and on the extent of the assignment. Ideally, the consultant is employed to begin work in the preparatory steps and continues through the completion of the working drawings, perhaps even through actual construction. He/she will assist in the writing of the building statements, in site selection, perhaps in selecting the architect, in schematic drawings, and in furniture and equipment layout sketches; and will attend important decision-making meetings and be available for consultations at any time.

Suggestions for selection of a consultant can be obtained from some issues of ALA's *American Libraries* and its publication *Library Building Consultant List.*[11] Although ALA does not indorse nor certify the 40 or so individuals listed, the purpose as stated in the introduction is "to provide librarians who are involved in building or renovation projects with a list of impartial consultants who have wide experience in all aspects of library building and design." Also there are companies that offer consultant services. These have the advantages of providing advice from a team of experts.

Although in many science library situations the selection of the architect for the entire building project will have already been made, in others the librarian may have some influence on the choice. Hopefully, the architect would have had successful experience in planning other libraries and, particularly, other comparable libraries. He must be willing to understand the requirements of his client, to comprehend how the library functions in the whole organization it serves, to study the building statement and respond to it with appropriate suggestions, and to plan a functional operation in architecturally pleasing quarters. The American Institute of Architects' national headquarters in Washington, D.C., and its comparable state organizations, can provide much help in selection and in relationships with the architect. The article How to Work with an Architect by Myron E. Lewis and Mark L. Nelson in the September 1982 issue, pages 44-46, of *Wilson Library Bulletin*[12] has much pertinent information on working relationships between client and architect.

These initial steps in preparing the way are not as distinct and separate as may be implied above. Rather they surely will overlap, and their order may be changed, but all must be included in a building project.

## WRITING A BUILDING PROGRAM STATEMENT

A building program statement has flexibility; that is, the objectives, functions and other elements are ideas and plans expressed in words that can easily be revised or completely changed. As a program materializes into sketches, preliminary and working drawings, and finally construction, changes become increasingly costly and difficult to make. Consequently, the written program is a most important element in the whole building schedule. Management and administration, team members, other library staff members, clientele and consultant can all be involved in the development process at this time. The final revision of the program will tell the architect what the library facility will accommodate and what functions it must serve. Requiring the architect to read the program once a week during the development stages would not be out of line.

In the program will be included information about library objectives and the library's place in the whole organization, about the site or location of the library, about furnishings, control, and space requirements of materials, services, readers and staff. With the inclusion of these elements the document becomes a basic part of the planning process. They are discussed in some detail in the rest of the article.

## PRELIMINARY BASIC DECISIONS

Planning a new facility or remodelling an old offers an unusual opportunity of examining how successful the library is serving its parent organization, what are its limitations and shortfalls, how the new facility can improve services. A clear statement of the ideal in the form of objectives will help to provide a base on which to plan. Included must be an evaluation, a priority established of objectives, as seldom is a facility planned without compromises, usually because of financial or space availability considerations.

The relationship with the organization served is a close one. The objectives of the library must be the same as, or must clearly support, the objectives and goals of the organization.

A decision must be made on the location of a new facility. If the library is to be a separate structure, or is to be assigned an area within a building, it should be located where the clientele will find it most convenient to use and where mail and other deliveries can conveniently be made. A center location in a building or in a complex of buildings is preferable to a peripheral location far away from those who will use the library. Another requirement of a good location is that it must allow for the expansion of the library into immediately adjacent space. Although some science libraries are static—no growth in services or materials—consideration should generally be given to space requirements for 5 to 10 years or perhaps more from time of completion. These projections are difficult to make but can be based on past growth figures of the library and of the organization. Adjacent office space separated from the library by non-load bearing walls is potential expansion room. The live load bearing factors of the floors must also be taken into consideration: 150 pounds per square foot for bookstacks, 175 pounds per square foot for compact storage and map cases, and 60 pounds per square foot for readers.

Perhaps many science and technology libraries functioning as part of a large organizational structure, and housed in a building with multiple components of the organization, do not have much to say about fixed function or flexibility, floor loads, ceiling heights, air conditioning, lighting and acoustics, and yet because they are all part of a successful setting for a library operation, they are indeed very relevant.

Planning flexibility for a library facility means having as few fixed, practically immovable, elements in the library as possible. As stairways, elevators, plumbing are among the fixed location items, they should be placed together in what may be called the core of the building. Other elements such as non-load bearing interior walls, and free standing book shelves, files and desks allow for flexibility in arrangement of services and materials. The live load factors for floors mentioned above must, of course, be taken into account. A uniform over-all lighting pattern may be planned, or light intensity and quality may vary, depending on the requirements of the activity served.[13] There are differences of opinion about what foot-candles and what quality of light are best. Electrical outlets on walls and in the floor must be sufficient to provide for typewriters, electric erasers, and reading, video cassette and phono machines; and some must allow for the use of equipment, such as copying machines that require 220 volts. Obviously lighting and outlets as related to flexibility must be considered.

Fortunately, the same air conditioning, temperature and humidity control is about equally satisfactory for people and most books and other library materials: in the neighborhood of 70° temperature and 45° to 55° humidity. However, special consideration must be made for rare books, precious manuscripts and similar items that require for preservation cooler temperatures, filtered air, and sensitive controls.

The librarian may have more input in the acoustical treatment than in some other features of the library area. Because of the library's services to the whole community, and because in some organizations it is a meeting center for staff and a show place for guests, it is allowed special treatment. High shelves with books and ceiling tiles absorb much sound. Also carpeting is an especially good acoustical treatment of floors as it prevents and absorbs noises, and in addition sets a tone or atmosphere immediately noticeable by people entering. A carpeted floor is as easy to maintain, and thought by some to be less costly, as a rubber, linoleum or vinyl tile covered floor.

In the planning of any facility attention should be given to making the library with its services and collections available to blind and physically handicapped individuals. By being aware of requirements and specifications for the slope of ramps, ways of improving access to the circulation desk, reading areas, bookstacks, etc., access can be built into the plans. Public Law 90-480, the Architectural Barriers Act of 1968, requires that buildings constructed or leased whole or in part with federal funds must be made accessible to and useable by the physically handicapped. Ruth A. Velleman's book *Serving Physically Disabled People*[14] covers the subject very well, and *Planning Barrier Free Libraries*, [15] a publication of the National Library Service for the Blind and Physically Handicapped of the Library of Congress, includes requirements, specifications with diagrams, and a checklist relevant to any library even though the publication concerns libraries designed specifically to serve handicapped individuals. Some states also adopted standards in this field and published documents about compliance and implementation. An example of this type of publication is *Accessibility Standards Illustrated*[16] of the State of Illinois Capital Development Board.

The librarian will probably have little influence about the type of construction to be used in the building unless the library is to be housed in a separate building. However, a modular building, one made up of uniform size square or rectangular bays, with dimensions to accommodate a maximum number of three-foot sections of shelving is economical to construct, has few interior obstructions and allows for a maximum amount of flexibility.[17]

Although final decisions will probably not be made until later in the planning process, it is advisable to consider the furniture and equipment to be used in the new facility as they are related to the building arrangement and design. The items that are fixed or attached to the structure itself are usually to be furnished by a general contractor who does the building. Other items, "loose" furniture and equipment, are separated from the general contract, may be included on some of the architectural drawings, but must be ordered separately.

Helpful information on furnishings are found in books and articles on general library planning, and much more specific and detailed help is available in William S. Pierce's *Furnishing the Library*,[18] published in 1980. For furniture and equipment he presents methods of selection and purchasing, information about manufacturing and marketing, as well as a general view of space planning and theory. Many illustrations and drawings assist the user to understand this rather technical material.

Before beginning work on specific and detailed requirements to be included in the program the librarian and other members of the team must know the amount of funds to be available for construction or know how many square feet of floor space will be allotted to the library. What are the limits within which the library must be planned? Effort is wasted if the project plans are way out of scope according to funds or space that management is willing to assign to the project.

With these statements and decisions ranging from the definition or role of the library to the financial or business limitations in hand, the next phase of planning can get under way.

## SPECIFIC CONSIDERATIONS AND REQUIREMENTS

Within the building program must be included space requirements for perhaps the next five or more years based on rate of past growth, current status and projections of future growth for the following:

—Materials: book and non-book
—Readers or users
—Library staff: technical processing, reader services, administration
—Library services: reference, research, circulation, interlibrary loan

Another approach to projecting building requirements suggested by Meredith Bloss is to plan the space in "user-oriented terms of the particular library, and in relation to the other service units in the community."[19] Bloss' idea is like zero budgeting in that the librarian begins with "user results, outputs, effectiveness, and satisfaction," rather than the existing status. Further, this theory calls for examining what other libraries in the community or field are doing and planning, recognizing the interdependence of libraries, and then determining how the new library is to be planned.

Whatever methods are used in projecting requirements, growth must be accepted as a foregone conclusion. The output of publications in all forms in science and technology continues to flood the market; research becomes more complex, sophisticated and multiple disciplinary; and the speed of scientific breakthroughs continues to increase.

To project the space needs for the library's holdings, a count of all its books, bound journals and any other publications shelved as books must be made and a measurement made of the running feet of shelf space for standard size books and for oversize volumes used to accommodate this material. Attention must be paid to the height of the volumes as bound journals and many reference books generally require more space in height and width than the usual monograph. By examining the annual rate of growth in each category over the last five years, a projection of future growth can be estimated. With this information—currently used shelving, space needed for growth and for allowances to assure a comfortable working shelving situation (perhaps one-third to one-fourth vacant) —a projected need for book shelving can be made. By converting these figures into standard single-faced shelving, three feet wide by 7½ feet high, the square feet of floor space needed can be projected either by an actual diagram or by referring to various formulas. Metcalf has included a most useful summary of formulas and tables as an appendix in his book referred to above.[20] The use of mobile shelving for storing books to save floor space is explained by Martin H. Collier in his article on the sixth stack addition at the University of Illinois. He projects with mobile shelving to house 28.4 volumes per square foot of floor area compared with 12.1 volumes per square foot for existing fixed shelving.[21] *Planning the Special Library*, edited by Ellis Mount, includes on pages 59-79 a comprehensive checklist to be used in formulating a program and in determining details of space capacities and requirements.[22] Bookstack manufacturers also provide information on capacities.

Similar analyses and projected square footage space requirements can be made for other library holdings: current and unbound journals, technical reports, maps, archives, vertical file materials, newspapers, fine arts, slides, microforms, cassettes, tapes, etc. Although these estimates are difficult to make and probably not extremely accurate, they do provide a base figure from which to work.

Projecting the number of readers or users to be accommodated is also difficult, but the experience of the library as well as the growth and direction of the organization served are significant factors. It should be remembered that a new, modern and comfortable facility is likely to attract more users. Then a determination must be made in placing the seats in the library, and in selecting what type of seating is to be used. The square footage required for each reader may vary from 20 square feet to a generous 35 where lounge chairs or individual tables are to be used.[23] The old library tables seating six or even eight are no longer used; rather a variety of tables seating a maximum of four to smaller tables seating one (with a large enough surface to allow for the spreading out of materials) are to be used.

The space requirements of the staff must also be projected. The requirements may differ from staff member to staff member, but formulas do exist to assist in making projections. Space occupied in the old quarters may well not be realistic to use in this projection as staff offices and work areas are notoriously overcrowded. Experience has proved that a library usually first runs out of staff space. For the current and each additional staff member anticipated 100 to 125 square feet should be allowed. Because of the location of offices near service points, adding space later to them and changing their location is usually not feasible.

Space should also be planned for staff conferences and meetings, perhaps in connection with the chief librarian's office, and for a staff lounge.

Adequate space must be provided for the card catalog. Except in very large libraries this projection should be made by considering the size of the current catalog, its projected growth rate as related to the growth of the collection, and the type or size of catalog to be used. A sketch with location of units may be helpful in visualizing the layout. For space requirements of catalog cards and their cases in a large library, situation formulas may prove helpful.[24] Of course, if an online computer-based catalog exists or is to be a part of the library's near future, requirements change, but space must be allowed. The number of CRT terminals depends on the volume of traffic expected. The same is true for microfiche catalogs and readers.

The circulation area must allow space for the desk itself, space for users to carry out transactions and for staff to carry on their related work. In a large system the circulation librarian would need an office. As most libraries now have some kind of mechanical if not automated circulation system, provisions must be made for the special equipment, and electric outlets and conduits. Depending on the workload, the interlibrary loan librarian may require a separate office.

The reference service area must allow room for the reference desk and staff on duty, for a small collection of reference books and for clientele seeking information. In order to prevent the inquirer from having to bend over to talk with the librarian, a desk of counter height is preferable. The square footage required for the activity will depend on the volume of traffic.

In many science and technology libraries parent organizations provide peripheral services—receiving and shipping, storage, janitorial rooms, public washrooms, etc.—but in one way or another they must be made available to the library. Metcalf includes as an appendix in his book "List of Equipment That Might Be Overlooked."[25] Again a reference to the extensive checklist in *Planning the Special Library* referred to above is in order. These are extremely useful lists to check.

Affecting all that has been discussed—collections, readers, staff accommodations, and services—is the certainty that many libraries are deeply into automation or will be. As material outside a library can more easily be located through online connections to databanks, such as OCLC, and thus, more easily borrowed, the size of the collection may be limited. For reference purposes the library's terminal can have access to millions of references to journal articles, government and industrial reports, conference papers, newspaper stories, patents and books. One commercial company alone has in its databank over 55 million such references. As databanks cover all major disciplines, they influence in one way or another most library collections. In locating computer terminals in the library the extremes of too much traffic and of too much isolation should be avoided. Convenient locations, but out of the main streams of traffic, are best. Ready access to cataloging information also affects the size of staff in technical services and in space requirements. Location and number of terminals must be considered in planning facilities for technical services. Margaret Beckman in her paper "Library Buildings in the Network Context," read at the 1982 IFLA Conference in Montreal, states that new technologies will decrease the rate of growth of collections in Canadian libraries as they depend more on networks.[26] She also tells of the influence of terminals, modems, printers and microcomputers on space allocations, and suggestions that even 175 square feet per staff member involved may be insufficient.

How the library is to participate in the application of the new technologies may be difficult to determine, but it is an important planning factor that must be taken into consideration in both reader and technical services areas.

## RELATIONSHIPS OF ACTIVITIES

With the determination of space requirements for housing materials and for readers and staff, the next step is to describe for the architect in the program how these are to be incorporated in his planning. The relationship of services will determine, to a large part, their location. Diagrams will help to show the flow of materials, work and traffic. But before considering this relationship, control and security must be examined.

The layout should be as simple as possible and, where feasible, duplicated on multifloor libraries. Persons at service desks should be able to indicate locations without recourse to complex diagrams and instructions. Vistas should be clear. The facility should be designed so as to minimize patrolling by staff. For example, views should be down aisles, not blocked by crosswise shelving and some partitions should be made of glass or have vision panels.

Only one exit should be provided, with the circulation desk located nearby. It is quite possible with careful planning to combine at the circulation desk the functions of exit control and circulation. Also the placement of this activity and the bookstacks is important. At the exit, in order to provide for the security of the collection, space and electric outlets are needed to accommodate a book theft detection system, such as Checkpoint or Tattle-Tape, and an entrance-exit turnstile in large libraries may be necessary. In many libraries control of the collection and general security are major problems. Some science libraries must be open at all times, even when no staff members are on duty, to serve the research staffs. Under these circumstances complete security becomes almost impossible. However, planning a new facility provides an opportunity to alleviate some of these problems.

Within the library users should have complete freedom to move about in all areas and to take books from one area to another, but the library must be so planned that as people leave they will pass close to a desk for outgoing traffic, where books to be taken out will be signed out. The flow of outgoing traffic, its relationship to incoming traffic, should be carefully studied and planned.

The reference or information counter should be visible and clearly marked for persons entering the library. When a person gets to the counter, he should be able to see the reference books, the public catalog, at least some of the books and other materials for circulation, and a reading area. The public catalog should be conspicuous and readily accessible not only to persons at reference, but also to persons in the circulation area and to technical services personnel.

Technical processes of acquisitions, cataloging, binding and repair of library materials constitute the behind-the-scenes operations of the library. Library materials must flow easily from receiving and mailing, to acquisitions, to cataloging, and finally to the book shelves. Technical process activities can be accommodated in one large open area divided by use of shelving if some demarcation is wanted. Besides the electrical outlets mentioned above, the area must have a sink with running water, counter top, and storage cabinets. Because of the necessity of having large quantities of processing materials on hand, it may be desirable to have the library's main supply storage closet here.

Perhaps it would be helpful to think of the users' areas of the library divided into three zones: one of main traffic, including the noises surrounding circulation and reference; next a semi-quiet area for using reference materials and current journals and papers; and finally a quiet zone of carrels and studies for use of researchers.

To have all these activities and materials logically located one to another is no simple assignment. The description of functions and requirements of the library making up the program statement will help to direct the planning process, but only after studying and criticizing many sketches, blue prints, or black-on-whites will the planning team and architect be ready to give their final approvals to proceed with the working drawings.

## REFERENCES

1. *Library Literature, 1933/35.* New York: H. W. Wilson; 1936-  .

2. Metcalf, Keyes D. *Planning academic and research library buildings.* New York: McGraw-Hill; 1965. 431 p.

3. Thompson, Godfrey. *Planning and design of library buildings.* 2d ed. London: Architectural Press; 1977. 189 p.

4. Mason, Ellsworth D. *Mason on library buildings.* Metuchen, NJ: Scarecrow; 1980. 333 p.

5. Mount, Ellis, ed. *Planning the special library.* New York: Special Libraries Association; 1972. 122 p. SLA Monograph no. 4.

6. Fox, Bette-Lee; Rosenthal, Shiri; Bock, D. Joleen. Library buildings in 1981. *Library Journal.* 106 (21): 2277-2286; 1981 December 1.

7. Fox, Bette-Lee; Burns, Ann; Waithe, Deborah. Library buildings in 1982. *Library Journal.* 107 (21): 2219-2229; 1982 December 1.

8. Selmer, Mirsha L. Draft standards for university map libraries. SLA Geography and Map Division. *Bulletin.* 129: 2-4; 1982 September.

9. *Library Trends.* 31 (1); 1982 Summer.

10. Dodd, James Beupré. The gap in standards for special libraries. *Library Trends.* 31 (1): 85-91; 1982 Summer.

11. ALA, Library Administration and Management Association, Buildings and Equipment Section. *Library buildings consultant list.* Chicago: ALA; 1982. 31 p.

12. Lewis, Myron E.; Nelson, Mark L. How to work with an architect. *Wilson Library Bulletin.* 57 (1): 44-46; September 1982.

13. Metcalf. p. 181-188; Thompson. p. 139-146; Mason. p. 25-38.

14. Velleman, Ruth A. *Serving physically disabled people, an information handbook for all libraries.* New York: Bowker; 1979. 392 p.

15. National Library Service for the Blind and Physically Handicapped. *Planning barrier free libraries.* Washington: Library of Congress; 1981. 61 p.

16. Illinois, Capital Development Board. *Accessibility standards illustrated.* Springfield, IL: The Board; 1978. 217 p.

17. Metcalf. p. 388.

18. Pierce, William S. *Furnishing the library interior.* New York: Dekker; 1980. 288 p.

19. Bloss, Meredith. Field/performance theory applied to library space planning. *In:* Nyren, Karl, ed. *Library space planning.* New York: Bowker; 1976: p. 52-54. LJ special report # 1.

20. Metcalf. p. 387-398.

21. Collier, Martin H. Sixth stack addition. *Library Journal.* 107 (21): 2235-2237; 1982 December 1.
22. Mount, ed. p. 59-79.
23. Metcalf. p. 392.
24. Metcalf. p. 396-397.
25. Metcalf. p. 399-402.
26. Beckman, Margaret. Library buildings in the network context. Mimeo. Paper presented at 48th IFLA general conference, Montreal: 1982. 16 p.

## ADDITIONAL REFERENCES

Anthony, L. J. Library planning. *In:* Ashworth, W., ed. *Handbook of special librarianship and information work.* 3rd ed. London: ASLIB; 1967: p. 309-364.

Cohen, Aaron; Cohen, Elaine. *Designing and space planning for libraries, a behavioral guide.* New York: Bowker; 1979. 250 p.

Lyles, Marjorie Appleman. Environmental design applications. *Special Libraries.* 63 (11): 495-501; 1972 November.

Mount, Ellis. *University science and engineering libraries, their operations, collections, and facilities.* Westport, CT: Greenwood Press; 1975. 214 p.

Schell, Hal B., ed. *Reader on the library building.* Englewood, CO: Microcard Editions Books; 1975. 359 p.

# Remodelled Library Facilities of the Oregon Regional Primate Research Center

### Isabel G. McDonald

**ABSTRACT.** The relocating of a small biomedical library to renovated larger quarters is reported. The conversion and move took four months and was accomplished with limited funds.

## *INTRODUCTION*

Nikas[1] has pointed out that "special libraries must adapt themselves to architecture not basically planned for their needs." In 1981, the library of the Oregon Regional Primate Research Center was enlarged and relocated to an area that previously contained its own storage area, the facilities of the Data Processing Department, the Medical Illustration Department, and four administrative offices (Figure 1).

The Oregon Regional Primate Research Center was established in 1960 by the National Institutes of Health as the first of seven centers. The library, as one of the earliest services in August 1961, had occupied an attractive location in the Administration Building. Its space included 1,575 sq.ft. on the upper level (main floor) of this two story building, plus a small storage area (J) (Figure 1) on the lower level.

The library serves a user population of about 170 employees, of which 35 are scientists. Its facilities are also occasionally used by faculty and students of the nearby Oregon Graduate Center. It

Isabel McDonald is the Librarian, Oregon Regional Primate Research Center, 505 N.W. 185th Ave., Beaverton, OR 97006. She holds a BA degree from the University of British Columbia and a BLS degree from the University of Toronto.

The author wishes to acknowledge the expert help of Mary Tobias, Katie Simon and Harry Wohlsein in the illustrations contained in this article.

*21*

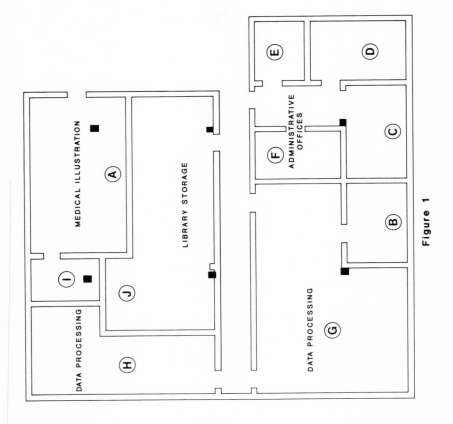

Figure 1

presently houses over 14,000 books and periodicals. Its subscriptions number 235. Equipment includes microfilm and microfiche reader/printers and one computer terminal. It has a small collection of historical primatology. The staff consists of 1.2 FTE professionals and 1.2 subprofessionals.

## BACKGROUND

The library had outgrown its shelving and its total space by 1976. By 1981 it had approximately 2,000 more volumes than its shelving could accommodate. Various expediencies had been used to house this growing collection, but the double shelving of volumes had become critical and dangerous.

In December 1979, the decision was made to relocate the library collection totally on the lower level of the building. During 1980, space would be freed by the move of Medical Illustration (I), (A) to a new Auditorium Building. Because of its new small computer, Data Processing (H),(G),(B) would move to a 40% smaller area on the same floor. By amalgamating the library on one level, the director would be able to consolidate his administrative staff in one location, the original library.

## PROBLEMS

Problems with the existing library were lack of space for collection, insufficient reader space and inadequate work space. There were no offices, no work rooms and no photocopier. The major problem of the new location was lack of shelving and funds to purchase it. Other considerations regarding the new site included 6 pillars, ceilings of various heights, a noisy, hollow-sounding computer floor, water leakage from windows, access to a staircase, and distance from the mail room. The only elevator was a slow freight elevator. As with the shelving, there would be no money for additional desks, chairs, filing cabinets, new circulation complex, nor funds to move the collection.

## PLANNING

No timetable had been set, but the librarian began to visit libraries of similar size and those that had moved recently. In addition she sought help in the library literature.[2,3,4]

We had previously consulted a movable shelving company representative who had drawn up plans for various areas in anticipation of hoped for funding. A library furniture representative drew up a most attractive plan, but one that did not allow for the size of the collection. A staff member drew up preliminary plans. In the fall of 1980, we engaged a local consultant for a modest fee to prepare a layout. She prepared an excellent floor plan, adding to it gummed cutouts representing shelving and existing furnishings. These could be adjusted if we wished to modify the layout. Recommendations for solutions to the problem of the computer floor were appended. At this time, the Medical Illustration service offered to build to scale a model of the consultants's plan, including the colors of walls and carpet we desired. Blocks built to scale as units of shelving were extremely helpful in envisioning the library three-dimensionally. The model was approximately 3′ × 3′.

The consultant's plan was not ultimately used because it was based on alterations previously agreed upon but later found to be too expensive. When we learned that alternate plans would have to be made, it was a simple matter to alter the walls in the scale model. This model generated much interest on the part of non-library personnel who volunteered several different arrangements. In the end, we drew up our own layout, a compromise of various plans, with small improvements being made at the time of the major move.

The most critical problem was lack of adequate shelving for the existing collection. Additional shelving was crucial to any plan. We were unable to find appropriate used shelving. After all avenues of possible funding had been exhausted, the librarian proposed using funds from the library's book budget to purchase shelving for the new storage area (A). Approval was given by the National Institutes of Health. (See Figure 2.)

The new storage room (A) was approximately 1/3 smaller than the old area (J). It had two doors, an outside wall and a pillar. We ignored the inside door between areas (A) and (I). By using the door to the hall, we would have access to the collection during

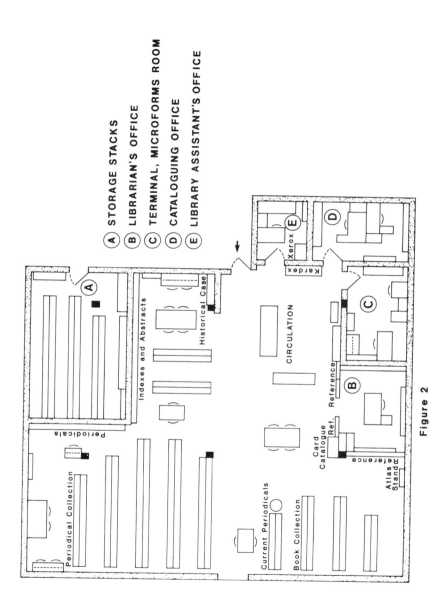

- (A) STORAGE STACKS
- (B) LIBRARIAN'S OFFICE
- (C) TERMINAL, MICROFORMS ROOM
- (D) CATALOGUING OFFICE
- (E) LIBRARY ASSISTANT'S OFFICE

Figure 2

25

the demolition of walls. In the newly renovated facility, the distance from the circulation desk would be shorter. Because of the physical constraints, we purchased narrow shelving and allowed less than standard aisles. We selected Aurora doublefaced steel shelving 18″ wide and planned the aisles at 27″. Delivery would take 6 weeks.

## THE MOVE

The relocation had to be managed in three phases. Phase 1 was the installation of new shelving in area (A), and the weeding and shifting of the collection in area (J) to area (A). Before Phase 2, a 6-week period intervened during which walls were demolished, leaks were corrected, heating and air conditioning ducts were relocated, tiles of the computer floor were stabilized and levelled, improvements to lighting and ventilation were made, walls were painted and carpeting was installed.

Phase 2 was the major move from upper level to lower level. The released shelving from old area (J) became the additional shelving we needed to keep ahead. Two library staff members and occasional volunteers gingerly unloaded top heavy shelves and transported volumes by library trucks using the freight elevator. Two library staff members reshelved volumes in the new location. The Physical Plant provided 5 men to dismantle shelving, reassemble it and move heavy furniture. In the new location, ends of stacks were placed a few inches from outside walls. At this time, the steel shelving was doubly or triply braced overhead with steel beams. The move took 4 days, one day less than expected. For the next 6 weeks we cohabited with administrative staff in rooms (C), (D) and (E) until the former library could be renovated for the consolidated administrative staff. After these rooms were vacated, they were painted and carpeted.

Phase 3 was moving furniture into these areas. It was accomplished in 45 minutes with no adjustments necessary to a plan carefully prepared by one of the library staff. Phase 4 consisted of re-shifting the entire periodical collection to allow for growth room where needed most.

## COSTS

The shelving cost our book budget $5,779. We saved the additional cost of installation by having the Physical Plant personnel assemble the shelving. Our consultant's fee was $100. Alterations to windows, lighting, wiring, heating and ventilation, and painting were carried out by Center personnel. Funding from the National Institutes of Health of $11,517 paid for paint, a door, miscellaneous alteration materials, carpeting and its installation, and removal of walls and computer room air ducts.

## THE FACILITY

The new facility (Figure 2) meets our needs well. We gained the additional shelving so absolutely necessary for the logistics of the move, and at the same time, enough for 4 to 5 years' growth. We enlarged our size from 1,878 sq.ft. to 3,250 sq.ft. Although we gained no additional seating, the new arrangement affords readers more working space and privacy. The library staff now has good working space. The circulation complex designed especially for the original library had to be broken apart. The separate components now frame a circulation "room" that has a feeling of openness but can be reduced in size as space is required for future shelving. Space for additional shelving was designed into the plan. The new shelving in storage area (A) is a component of Spacesaver movable shelving and can be converted in later years. All staff offices (B),(D),(E) have good visual control and are close to the library entrance. Telephones are located in these rooms, at the back of the circulation area, and on the pillar in what had been room (I).

Room (E) is a small crowded office (10′ × 10′) which would have been larger were we designing a library. However it functions well. Room (C) with its pillar offered the poorest visual control, and so was planned as the microforms and terminal room. This equipment is centrally located and easily accessible to its many users. Wiring for additional terminals was installed. The location of indexes and abstracts in old area (J) is much more accessible to

FIGURE 3.

the interlibrary loan staff member than it had been in the former library. This corner of the library, near the entrance, is one of the most attractive areas of the library. The card catalog was placed near the book collection for the convenience of users and library staff.

The walls, painted either blond yellow or antique white, give a sunny appearance at all times despite the small windows 7'3" above the floor. An outside ledge extending beyond the tops of the windows seems to buffer the light so that the quality is pleasant and even. A glass door on an outside wall located near the current periodicals also provides light. The main door to the library is glass with a wooden frame. (See Figure 3.)

## SUCCESS OF THE FACILITY

The minor losses are the convenient access to the mail room and a beautiful view. The gains are multitudinous. The library staff is pleased with the new library facility and its layout. After 18 months we have made no changes. The total appearance is much more attractive than we envisioned. The lighting is excellent. We prefer it to the radiation experienced in the original library with its two outside walls of glass. The heating seems better regulated and is more comfortable. Our additional phone on the pillar is an extra convenience for the user as well as any staff member working in the periodicals area.

The Center's administration gave great support to the library during and after its relocation. The library acquired a photocopier from the upper level, a number of wooden bookcases from previous tenants, some desks and cabinets, and some large handsome plants that have thrived in the new location.

The most unexpected response was the return of several scientists to personal use of the library. The long staircase between the upper and lower floors has not deterred use. Despite a disrupted 4-month period between Phases 1 and 3, and despite a reduction of 15-20% in Center personnel, our circulation statistics for 1981 were 15% higher than in 1980.

We believe that we have made significant improvements to our library facility with extremely limited funds.

# REFERENCES

1. Nikas, Mary. Interior design: beauty is our excuse. *In*: Mount, Ellis, ed. *Planning the special library*. New York: Special Libraries Association; 1972: p.22.

2. Cohen, Aaron and Cohen, Elaine. *Designing and space planning for libraries: a behavioral guide*. New York: Bowker; 1979.

3. Mount, Ellis, ed. *Planning the special library*. New York: Special Libraries Association; 1972.

4. Thompson, Godfrey. *Planning and design of library buildings*. 2d ed. London: Architectural Press Ltd.; New York: Nichols Publishing Co.; 1977.

# Adapting Non-Library Facilities for Periodical Collections at Brookhaven National Laboratory

Ken Ryan
Marilyn Galli

**ABSTRACT.** In order to cope with space limitations and rapidly growing periodical collections, Brookhaven National Laboratory Research Library undertook to investigate the use of various "recycled" non-library facilities to be used as a library annex. Several interim solutions are discussed and details of a low-cost use of industrial shelving in a former chapel/theatre are given. Advisory support from plant engineers and architects, as well as from a library user advisory committee, was shown to be essential in arriving at a viable and cost-effective solution to a serious space problem.

## INTRODUCTION

Brookhaven National Laboratory (BNL) is operated by Associated Universities, Inc. (AUI) under a contract with the United States Department of Energy (DOE). The Laboratory conducts a broad range of basic and applied research programs in the physical and life sciences. It occupies a 21-km$^2$ tract of land (5,265 acres) at Upton, NY, approximately at the geographic center of Long Island, about 100 kilometers east of New York City.

AUI was formed in 1946 by a group of nine universities[1] for the purpose of establishing and managing BNL and other research cen-

Ken Ryan is Manager, Technical Information Division, and Marilyn Galli is Administrator, Research Library, both at Brookhaven National Laboratory, Upton, New York 11973. The authors would like to thank Robert C. Stauber of the Plant Engineering Division of BNL for his highly creative and enthusiastic approach to recycling buildings for library use. The authors would also like to thank Dr. H. William Siegelman of the Biology Department of BNL whose indefatigable efforts as Chairman of the Research Library Advisory Committee paid off for all of us. This work has been performed under Contract No. DE-AC02-76H00016 with the United States Department of Energy.

ters. This action represented a new approach to the management of fundamental research with the support of the Federal government, especially for large-scale scientific enterprises of importance to the academic community.

From 1947 to 1975 the Laboratory was supported by the U.S. Atomic Energy Commission. In 1975 the Atomic Energy Commission was abolished and most of its research programs were taken over by the Energy Research and Development Administration, which in 1977 was incorporated into the newly created Department of Energy. The U.S. Nuclear Regulatory Commission, which was formed in 1975 to take over the regulatory functions of the AEC, supports a continuing program of studies at BNL on the safety of nuclear power reactors.

The Laboratory has an annual budget of over $200 million and employs over 3,000 people. At least one-third of this number are potential library users. BNL libraries cover the following scientific-technical subject areas, largely in support of the Laboratory's diversified research programs: applied mathematics; biology; chemistry; energy technology; environmental technology, safety, and protection; nuclear (reactor) safety; nuclear materials safeguards; nuclear waste management; medicine; high energy physics and particle accelerators; nuclear and atomic physics; and solid state physics. Collections are located in a number of facilities, including the (main) Research Library, several reading rooms (unstaffed), and several staffed departmental libraries. Collection statistics are summarized in Table 1.

The Research Library represents the core collection for BNL. Central cataloging and monographic and serials acquisition are performed by Research Library staff. Those departmental libraries staffed by professional librarians, as well as the Research Library, provide a full range of additional services to their users (often rather specialized groups of individuals), including ILL, photocopying, reference, online searching (BRS, DIALOG, ORBIT, DOE/RECON, NASA/RECON, NLM, etc.). Reading rooms are looked after by part-time secretarial staff in the departments in which the facilities are located. A considerable degree of cooperation exists among all the various library-related personnel on site; however, cooperation can go only so far under the pressing constraints of budgets and space. The following paragraphs consider one example of facility problems and attempted solutions at the Research Library at BNL.

Table 1

BNL Libraries Collection Statistics

Research Library

| Book volumes | 40,000 |
| Periodical titles | 900 |
| Bound volumes | 40,000 |
| Technical reports (print & microform) | 450,000 |

Other Facilities

| Book volumes | 20,000 |
| Periodical titles | 1,200 |
| Bound volumes | 20,000 |
| Technical reports (mostly print) | 70,000 |

## NEED FOR NEW FACILITY

One aspect of providing library services to the scientific-technical community is the continual and growing demand for coverage in the periodical and report literature. Accordingly, collection growth and space demands in these areas far exceed those of monographs. As a result, the Research Library's periodical stack areas began to overflow, forcing the current periodicals room to house several years of runs beyond its designed capacity; making it necessary to shelve binding shipments wherever there was room (typically, not in sequence and not in the main collection area); requiring users to be highly inventive and considerably patient in locating items; and forcing personnel to stack materials in the aisles and on under-shelf sliding reference trays in some areas. In addition, it was necessary to keep books in indefinite circulation since bound periodicals were encroaching on book collection space and causing serious overcrowding there.

As an initial step to solving this problem, library personnel identified a number of periodical titles which had become closed entries, largely as a result of budgetary cutbacks which forced cancellations. Nearly 425 periodical titles were shifted out of the main periodical stacks and into adjacent compact (movable, manually cranked) shelving. These latter units housed printed technical reports which themselves were being weeded of materials for which microfiche copies were available in-house. Printed journal back-runs had already been replaced with microfilm wherever possible, so further space reduction was not possible, especially considering the necessity to maintain viable sets of items for union list cooperation.

It was quickly noted, however, that valuable shelving in the major research information facility was being used to store titles which users and librarians, somewhat reluctantly, had decided were not of sufficient interest to justify their central location. Accordingly, it was decided to reserve shelves in the Research Library for the most active parts of the periodical collection and to relocate those inactive parts. Some experience had already been gained in weeding-to-storage in the monographic collection: about 2,000 titles had been removed, accounted for, boxed, and stored. That the weeding criterion (no circulation in 15 years) was reasonable is indicated by the recall rate: around 20 items in over two years, or less than one-half of one percent per year.

These periodical closed entries were removed and boxed in order to open up the shelves, to allow binding shipments to be merged into the collection, and to provide a more user-oriented (self-service) facility. Boxes were sequentially numbered and contents were noted on the outside. No special order of shelf removal was in effect, since title cards showing box numbers and volumes and years contained therein were prepared during the procedure. No notations were made on the periodicals holding file records since this boxing was to be a temporary measure. In addition to the approximately 425 closed entry titles, another 225 open entries were identified for partial removal. These titles, in general, had lengthy backruns which, it was felt, could be interrupted at an arbitrary cutoff date and storage arranged for volumes prior to that date.

It was virtually impossible to keep an accurate tally of the number of shelves vacated as the removal and boxing took place. Initial shelf counts for both closed and open entries totaled nearly 1,000 shelves, but this count was not updated during the boxing cycle. It was determined (from two sampling points) that 1.2 boxes were required to contain one shelf. Since 994 total boxes were packed, the shelf count was 828 (i.e., 994/1.2). Using an average journal (cubic) volume estimate and the volume of the boxes, a theoretical maximum figure of about 1,100 shelves was obtained. Thus the number of vacated shelves (and hence the number of shelves which must be replicated in another facility) ranged from 828 (computed from the box count and a reliable box-per-shelf factor) through about 1,000 (based on an initial shelf count which diminished during the packing as some titles were not removed) up to a theoretical maximum of about 1,100. The slight problems evident here point out the fact that an accurate shelf count is necessary.[2]

Boxes were constructed and packed in place in building corridors to facilitate removal to storage. Warehouse shelving was available for slightly under 400 boxes; space for stacking boxes in rows (three boxes high by two wide) was made available for an additional 300 plus boxes. The remaining nearly 300 boxes were left in library corridors. Obviously this "living-out-of-boxes" situation was less than desirable, especially from the standpoint of retrieving items to fill users' requests. Over a three-month period, approximately 350 volumes were retrieved, representing 18 shelves of material.

## *FACILITIES MADE AVAILABLE AND ADAPTATIONS FOR USE*

The extreme difficulty in retrieving materials stored in boxes stacked in a warehouse (on site, but remote), the unavailability of these items for browsing, the several days delay in obtaining a photocopy of a needed item, the frustration of librarians and users alike knowing that needed items were so near yet so far away, and a host of other negative points demanded a quick solution to the facility problem.

Additional library stack space had been proposed and approved, but it was destined to house the reference collection and be constructed around a user-oriented reference counter in the main reader area. The shelving made available from this shift was to be used to expand the abstract and index area, also suffering from space constraints. This shelving amounted to only 20 percent of the minimum required for the periodicals, so it could not be used for this function, even if it were available.

As an immediate solution, it was proposed to use a building recently vacated. Careful analysis of the structure showed that the flooring had been damaged by photographic chemical spillage over an extended period and therefore could not bear a book load. In addition, extensive wall rearrangement would be necessary, heating, ventilating, and air conditioning would require extensive (and expensive) modifications, and previous darkroom and task lighting systems would have to be altered to meet library stack requirements. This project was quickly abandoned. Fortunately, a much better solution was found instead.

Some curtailment of experimental programs freed veterinary service annex to the Medical Research Center at BNL, located several blocks from the Research Library. It had been "mothballed" for an indefinite period of time; however, it was strongly anticipated that programs would be resumed in three years, thus requiring all interim occupants to vacate. A solution to using a rather unconventional space and arrangement was devised as shown in Figure 1. The library facility would occupy about 60 percent of the total area; the remainder would be turned over to other users for storage. Modifications to the building included removal of a number of doors, installation of another door, and rerouting of some air conditioning ducting. The building was structurally ideal—well sealed, of block construction and with a concrete slab foundation—but its disadvantages included no large room(s), a need to modify (cut down) purchased shelf units to accommodate differing ceiling heights, and the previously mentioned short-term occupancy limitation. Plans for its adaptation proceeded, however.

Standard, high-grade industrial-type of shelving was selected. both 12- and 24-inch-deep units were purchased in order to make maximum use of the space. Table 2 shows the shelving tabulation. The A and B units vary one foot in height and are 24 inches deep. It was planned to shelve items one behind the other on 2-foot-deep shelves in order to double the lineal footage available in the shelving. Three rows could be accommodated if need be. The C and D units are 12 inches deep and, again, vary in height by one foot.

This arrangement would, of course, strain the user (note the shelf sequence shown in Figure 1). Indeed, it was planned that the annex would be primarily accessible only to library staff. A photocopier would be located there and trips would be made two or three times a week to locate and copy materials. Browsing would be severely curtailed; it was anticipated that only the heartiest user would brave the complexities of the proposed arrangement. However, the arrangement did provide nearly 1,400 shelves (recall that the estimated shelving needs ranged from over 800 to over 1,100), although growth room was not essential since items going into the

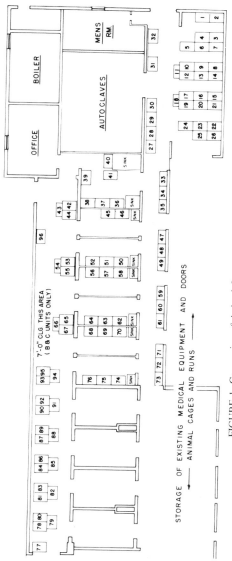

FIGURE 1. Conversion of Animal Quarantine Facility to Library Annex.

Table 2

Shelving Tabulation for Animal Quarantine Facility

| Type unit | Dim. (ft.) | Shelves (equiv.) | Linear ft./unit | Number of units | Total shelves | Total linear ft. |
|-----------|------------|------------------|-----------------|-----------------|---------------|------------------|
| A | 2 x 3 x 8 | 16 | 48 | 65 | 1040 | 3120 |
| B | 2 x 3 x 7 | 12 | 36 | 26 | 312 | 936 |
| C | 1 x 3 x 7 | 6 | 18 | 3 | 18 | 54 |
| D | 1 x 3 x 8 | 8 | 24 | 2 | 16 | 48 |
| | | | TOTALS | 96 | 1386 | 4158 |

area were either closed entries or early numbers of long backruns, and also the duration of occupancy was limited.

The combined costs for this conversion project were estimated to be about $12,500, with shelving accounting for approximately $7,500 and building modifications (labor and materials) and shelving setup (labor) accounting for the rest. It would have been challenging to use this facility. Indeed, the efficiency of using three shelving units in a U-shaped arrangement rather than a strictly linear arrangement in the upper corridor (refer to Figure 1) allowed nearly a 50 percent gain in shelving. Despite these improvements over the previous plan, this facility was viewed with displeasure by the large and vocal library user community, led by the library advisory committee. With their help, plans were once again altered and still a third building was chosen.

As noted by the library advisory committee, the facility finally agreed upon possessed the following advantages:

- Proximity to the (main) Research Library (across the street)
- An active building (not "mothballed")
- Previous use as library shelving area
- Existence of a more suitable facility for displaced occupants
- Long-term (i.e., "permanent") occupancy by Research Library

Architecturally, there were disadvantages as well as advantages. Since the facility had been a chapel and then a theatre, a high ceiling made possible future double-decking of industrial shelving. However, the pier-and-beam foundation would require new foot-

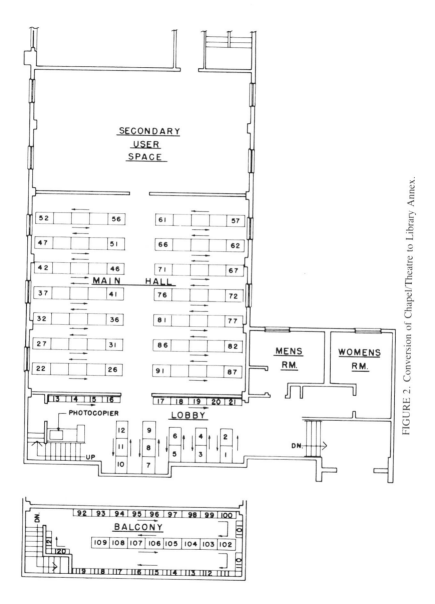

FIGURE 2. Conversion of Chapel/Theatre to Library Annex.

Table 3

Shelving Tabulation for Chapel/Theatre

| Area | Number of units | Shelves (equiv.) | Linear ft./unit | Total shelves | Total linear ft. |
|---|---|---|---|---|---|
| | | 24-inch Units | | | |
| Main Hall | 70 | 10 | 30 | 700 | 2100 |
| Lobby | 12 | 10 | 30 | 120 | 360 |
| Balcony | 8 | 8 | 24 | 64 | 192 |
| Total | 90 | – | – | 884 | 2652 |
| | | 12-inch Units | | | |
| Main Hall | – | – | – | – | – |
| Lobby | 9 | 5 | 15 | 45 | 135 |
| Balcony | 22 | 4 | 12 | 88 | 264 |
| Total | 31 | – | – | 133 | 399 |
| | | Totals | | | |
| | 121 | – | – | 1017 | 3051 |

ings to be poured for such double-decking. In fact, full vertical use of the shelving would not be possible because of floor loading safety factors. This limitation resulted in a net reduction in linear shelving footage of about 25 percent compared to the previous facility, and required the purchase of additional shelving units to make maximum use of the space. However, it would not be necessary to customize these units to fit varying ceiling heights as in the previous facility and so they would be completely recyclable. Some modifications to the construction of the units were required in order to convert to two-sided access in the new facility. Figure 2 shows the layout of the chapel/theatre facility; shelving tabulations are given in Table 3.

The combined costs for this conversion should not exceed $15,000, broken down as follows: $7,500 for shelving (as before) plus an additional $2,500 for more shelving units, different braces, footing plates (for use on wood vs. concrete floor), backs and sides (to prevent volumes from falling from the balcony); and, as before, about $5,000 for shelf erection and building modifications (extending an interior wall, altering light and heat controls to allow individual control over two separate areas, and installation of dehumidifiers to regulate environmental conditions in the summer). The facility was ready for occupancy by the end of 1982. As before, a photocopier will be provided in the building, which, although unstaffed, will have the same hours as the main library. Personnel currently responsible for shelf maintenance and demand photo-copying will perform the same functions in the annex.

## CONCLUSIONS

Two workable solutions to space problems by recycling build-ings designed for other uses have been discussed. The tradeoffs at BNL, in the long run, were centered around the user rather than utility. Whereas the more structurally sound second-proposed fa-cility would have provided one-third again as much linear shelving, the disadvantages of remoteness and a "user-snarly" shelving ar-rangement weighed heavily in making the final decision. Strong opinions expressed at the right management levels by a very sup-portive library committee made it possible to obtain the best "user-friendly" facility. Good support by plant engineering personnel for detailed design analysis was seen to be essential for planning the use of non-library facilities. Of course, the ultimate solution would be to design and build an attached annex to existing facilities, but under normal budgetary strictures, recycling of non-library build-ings is seen to be an economical and viable solution to library space problems.

## REFERENCE NOTES

1. Associated Universities, Inc. comprise Columbia University, Cornell University, Harvard University, Johns Hopkins University, Massachusetts Institute of Technology, Princeton University, University of Pennsylvania, University of Rochester and Yale Univer-sity.

2. Boxes used were 18 by 12 by 14 in. (1.75 cu. ft.). Several counts of the number of shelves making up a given number of boxes yielded the 1.2 boxes-per-shelf ratio. The volume of a typical periodical shelf actually occupied by material was needed to determine floor loading later in the project. Two 50-title samples were taken by measuring (to the nearest 1/8 in.) bound (cover) height and depth of an arbitrary range of periodicals. The average height was 10.14 in. and the depth 7.37 in. On a standard (36 in.) shelf, the volume occupied is therefore 1.56 cu. ft. The maximum storage volume in boxes is 1,739.5 cu. ft. (1.75 cu. ft. per box times 994). Therefore, 1,739.5/1.56 or 1,115 is the maximum number of shelves of average-sized periodicals which can be stored in the volume available. In a box volume of 2.1 cu. ft. (1.2 times 1.75) the equivalent volume of 1.56 cu. ft. of periodicals (i.e., one average shelf) was packed. This represents a utilization factor of about 75 percent (1.56/2.1), a measure of "packing efficiency."

# Design of Library Facilities
# for the Ontario Ministry
# of Transportation and Communications

Stefanie A. Pavlin
Guna Plumanis
Laila R. Zvejnieks

**ABSTRACT.** This article describes the history, planning, design and move of the Library & Information Centre of the Ontario Ministry of Transportation and Communications. It details some specific characteristics of library planning in a government environment.

## INTRODUCTION

The Library & Information Centre of the Ontario Ministry of Transportation and Communications (MTC) was created to serve the special information needs of Ministry staff. Its mandate has been expanded to include the transportation community in the area. Over the years the Library has developed into one of the finest transportation-oriented libraries in Canada with emphasis on ground transportation. Reference service emphasizes manual and online literature searching, interlibrary loan, SDI, current awareness, referral services and resource sharing. Requests for information are regularly received from across North and South America and Europe.

The staff of nine—four professional librarians and five library

Stefanie A. Pavlin is Head, Library Services, Library & Information Centre, Ontario Ministry of Transportation and Communications (M.T.C.), 1201 Wilson Avenue, Downsview, Ontario, Canada, M3M 1J8. She has a BA degree from Mt. St. Vincent University and a BLS degree from the University of Toronto. Guna Plumanis, who is Librarian, Reference Services, has a BJ degree from Carlton University and a BLS degree from the University of Toronto. Laila R. Zvejnieks, who is Serials and Indexing Librarian, has a BA degree from Heidelberg College and the MLS degree from Kent State University.

technicians—provides the above services in addition to acquisition of publications and subscriptions for the library as well as all MTC offices, five regions and eighteen districts throughout Ontario.

Satellite libraries were established over the years for special interest sections, such as the Legal Services, Communications Division, Ministry agencies and regional centers. Technical and advisory services for these libraries are provided from the Head Office Library. Staffing for satellite libraries is the responsibility of each section or agency.

## HISTORY

After World War II, Ontario embarked on a period of great road and bridge building activity. In the early 1950s a visionary engineer in the then Ontario Department of Highways (now MTC) decided that a library was needed to serve the Materials & Research laboratories and support the research activities of the department. A librarian was hired to develop a library for this section. The librarian worked with temporary clerical help for a while, but within a year two permanent library clerks were hired.

In 1960 a new building was opened to house the entire Department of Highways (D.H.O.). At this time it was decided to amalgamate the Materials & Research library and the many small collections of books scattered throughout various offices into a fully-organized library to serve the entire D.H.O. Approximately 1100 sq. ft. was allotted to the library. By 1969, the library was forced to move twice more to make space for other offices.

The last location was a windowless, poorly-ventilated, 24 × 84 ft. room never intended to house a library. The cataloging function and the reading room were located in separate adjoining areas and several vertical files were placed in a neighboring office. There was no direct access from a main corridor.

## NEED FOR NEW FACILITIES

In 1971, the already limited space was severely taxed when the Department of Highways and the Department of Transport merged to form the Department (now Ministry) of Transportation and Communications, and the two departmental libraries became one. All the Department of Transport materials, including shelving, were moved to the D.H.O. Library.

By 1973, staff had increased to ten. Desks were squeezed between stacks and books were crammed on top of shelves. The collection was also growing to meet expanding demands as the priorities of the Ministry changed. Holdings were approaching 50,000 volumes, and 800 serial titles. A new facility was desperately needed, but it took six more years until a suitable space was found.

Once again, in 1975 the library was requested to give up its space—this time for the expansion of an ever-growing computer facility. At that point the library became part of an overall renovation project for the entire East Building. The head librarian worked closely with a consulting architect. The purpose of the library was identified; all library services, including a computer terminal room, were considered; the needs for study and reading space were reviewed; work flow was studied; and the need for a separate work room was recognized. The architect proposed structural changes at the new location. The plan that evolved not only adequately provided for all library needs, but was also quite "glamorous" with plate-glass floor-to-ceiling windows, proper lighting, new custom-made furniture, display cabinets and plants scattered throughout. But it was not to be. The first fiscal constraints were in place. The library and the rest of the projected East Building renovations, were the first victims.

Two more years elapsed and additional constraints came along, threatening the library's very existence. The library complement of 10 was reduced to nine and some services had to be cut.

Hastily, a nine-member Library Users Advisory Committee was appointed by the Deputy Minister. This committee, jointly with the head librarian, studied the existing library service, space limitations and an inadequate budget. The committee then made a number of recommendations concerning additional library services, an increased budget and relocation of the library to larger quarters. Two suggested locations where space was available proved to be too small.

Finally an adequate space of 7,200 sq. ft. was offered on the ground floor of the Central Building which had housed the original Materials and Research library. The advantages of this location were: direct access from the main lobby of the building and from a connecting tunnel and cat-walks from the other three buildings; a multitude of windows running the length of two walls and adequate space, somewhat exceeding immediate requirements. Since the building was originally designed to accommodate testing laboratories, floors were already reinforced.

There were disadvantages as well that had to be considered, and a compromise had to be reached. The space offered to relocate the library was not in one area but in two rooms on the same floor divided by a lobby. The lighting was never designed for a library nor could it be changed. There were too many doors in both areas which could not be closed off due to fire regulations. Multiple support columns in both areas presented a problem with arrangement of stacks. Two circulation control desks had to be provided— one in each area, dividing the staff of nine, with three people staffing the periodicals area and six the reference area.

## PLANNING AND DESIGN

Since the now abandoned "glamorous" plan and the Library Users Advisory Committee had already defined the functions and services of the library, the planning for this newly assigned area could start at once. This time the professional advice of an architect was not available. All the planning and design had to be done by the head librarian and a Ministry planning officer.

The design of the new facility had to be rushed, as the library had to vacate its quarters immediately to make room for the expansion of the computer facility.

The guidelines for the layout and physical space requirements were those recommended by the Ontario Government Librarians Council (OGLC) in its report entitled "Library services in the Ontario government; today and tomorrow" (1973):

—staff work areas were to be 100-180 sq. ft. per function
—a minimum of 25-30 sq. ft. was to be allowed for individual study space
—25 sq. ft. per person was to be allowed for study tables that seat up to four people
—50 sq. ft. per person was to be allowed in the lounge area

—library circulation and reference areas (a basic service unit) was to consist of one circulation desk, one reference desk, one card catalogue, one reference book case, one typing stand and one book truck and was to be allotted 400 sq. ft.

—for the library collection 12 linear feet of shelving per 100 volume of books, 16 linear feet per 100 volumes of periodicals and 1-2 feet of lateral files per 100 reports was to be provided

—that provision for a five-year expansion was to be made.

It was decided that the existing shelving would be used in one area and that new shelving and new furniture would be ordered for the other area.

Because of the two locations, the decision was made to split the collection along "natural lines," separating serials from the book and reference collection.

The windows that were such a pleasant change turned out to be a problem as no shelving could be positioned against those walls. To solve the problem, six staff offices and the computer terminal area were located along the window walls.

Wall space between the numerous doors was utilized for carrels and study tables. Four support columns were furnished with bulletin boards for various announcements and releases. Shelving had to be positioned against the support columns to provide adequate aisle space. Spacing of the lights remained a problem. However, light from the windows partially compensated for this. A special intercom system had to be installed between the two locations.

Once the final plan was approved, the move had to be made, even though the new areas were not ready for occupancy and new shelving and furniture were still on order. (See Figure 1.)

## MOVING THE COLLECTION

The packing of boxes and labeling was done by library staff. In the new location, the staff again unpacked and organised the collection on temporary shelving. Part of the collection had to be left in boxes. This became an advantage, as the books had to be repacked and shelving moved in order to install the carpeting and paint the walls and ceiling (the staff did not participate in this undertaking). Books were again reshelved, so that service could be

FIGURE 1.

restored. Five long months later the new shelving and furniture arrived. This time the library collection was packed by professional library movers and stored in a moving van, which was parked on the Ministry parking lot for a week, until the new shelving was assembled and furniture arranged.

When the collection was unpacked and reshelved by the movers, it had to be rearranged by library staff, which took another ten days. After the move was completed, the problems of being in two locations began surfacing.

Part of the heavily used core collection had to be bound to form permanent reference copies and provide circulating copies e.g., Transportation Research Board publications, thus necessitating duplication of the collection and ensuring security. The catalogue and shelf list are located in the reference area while the kardex, used as a guide to serials, is located in the periodicals area. This necessitates tracking back and forth for acquisitions checking of library holdings.

FIGURE 2.

49

Staffing the two areas has not been a problem, due to careful planning of compressed and flexible work hours, vacations, attendance of meeting and professional development programs.

The colour of the carpeting and walls was not the responsibility of the library planners, as the maintenance and upkeep of all government buildings is coordinated by another Ministry. However, the library planners did select the furniture and shelving. To brighten the gold-brown carpet and charcoal brown walls, off-white furniture and shelving were selected. Several brass silk screen prints, and original oil and water colour paintings, depicting transportation themes, were selected from the in-house Art Design Section to enhance the walls. Large potted plants were found and placed throughout the two areas. Light oak, oatmeal coloured padded screens were used to divide staff work areas from public areas. New gold upholstered chairs complement the colour scheme. Bright, custom-made gold coloured signs indicate library activity areas, such as circulation and inquiry, reference, cataloguing and others. (See Figure 2.)

## COMMENTS

This may be considered an account of the planning and relocation of one particular library, but it should not be used as a model for other libraries planning a change. Because of rather rigid government guidelines, the MTC Library and Information Centre planners were limited in their choices and decisions.

In retrospect, we do not regret this "split decision." Staff cooperation and morale is excellent and users are frequenting the more spacious and pleasant quarters in greater numbers.

## REFERENCE

Ontario Government Librarians Council. *Library services in the Ontario government: today and tomorrow*. Toronto: 1973. 37 p.

# Library Facilities
# for the Riley Stoker Corporation

## Cosette M. Kotseas

**ABSTRACT.** The following paper outlines the planning of the Riley Stoker Corporation Library from its development in January 1979 to the present, serving the entire company in an area of approximately 400 square feet. A needs assessment, operational goals, space allocations, and budgetary data are included.

## *BACKGROUND*

Riley Stoker Corporation, established in 1913, is a pioneer in the field of steam generating and fuel burning equipment. Manufacturing power boilers, stokers, accessories, and coal pulverizing equipment with a major concern in environmental pollution; we currently employ 700 people at our home plant in Worcester, Massachusetts, including a separate R&D facility, manufacturing operations in Erie, Pennsylvania and Sapulpa, Oklahoma, and a nationwide sales force. Our foreign licensees selling Riley products abroad are located in France, Japan, and Australia.

Prior to the establishment of a library, vast quantities of technical information were accumulated by various departments. Secretaries were responsible for indexing and filing the literature. Three attempts were made at centralization when it was realized that a professional librarian was required in January, 1979. Priority was given to the hiring of a librarian and the centralization problem before a library location was actually found.

Cosette M. Kotseas, who received her MLS at Simmons College, is Information Specialist, Riley Stoker Corporation, P.O. Box 547, Worcester, MA 01613. The author wishes to thank Linda J. Lagerstrom, MLS, the former Riley librarian, for background information.

## *LIBRARY OBJECTIVES*

The establishment of a library was originally to serve the Engineering Division of Riley Stoker Corporation with the following objectives in mind: To provide more efficient access to the quantity of technical literature already owned by the division; to provide more efficient retrieval of information to be obtained outside the company; to consolidate the ordering of technical material, eliminating multiplication of effort; to reduce loss through better control; and to establish a central information facility for the division. Instrumental in planning were the librarian, the Vice President of Engineering, and Engineering Administration. Although the objectives remain the same, the library now serves the entire Riley community as opposed to the Engineering Division alone.

Examination of goals and problems indicated that the flow of information would benefit from the following programs:

a. Centralized ordering of all technical literature.
b. Reference service utilizing both Riley's collection and the facilities of neighboring libraries.
c. Introduction of computerized literature searching.
d. Designation of and provision of appropriate furnishings and equipment to a workable library area.
e. Inventory of widely scattered and poorly documented collection of technical literature.
f. Computerized cataloging of the collection.
g. Institution of controls on its use.
h. Encouragement of the use of microforms to save time and money.
i. Proper maintenance of an up-to-date collection of vendor catalogs and competitor information files.

## *SERVICES*

The library offers a wide range of services to its clientele. On-line literature searching is provided via Lockheed DIALOG and is widely used throughout the company. Access is provided through a Digital Decwriter IV in the Accounting Department. DIALOG was chosen mainly for its large number of searchable files, the simplicity and flexibility of its searching language, and the option of paying for only the service used without contracting in advance for a minimum amount. (See Figure 1.)

"Library Update," a monthly newsletter, is distributed to employees in Worcester, Erie, and Sapulpa. Featured are a news section, reference spotlight, and recent acquisitions. A bulletin board is located in the hallway outside of the library, posting literature pertaining to various conferences and seminars. Interlibrary loan service is offered and depended on greatly.

Although the library has no OCLC terminal, arrangements have been made to use the terminal at an area college for locating information. Standard LC forms are used, and copyright laws are followed. A list of our serial holdings is included in the *Worcester Area Cooperating Libraries Union List*.

Material is acquired on an "as needed" basis. The library will purchase any requested information provided that it can be cataloged and considered property of the library. Due to this practice, a fair amount of material is checked out on permanent loan. About 50% of our serials are routed and, with the exception of "Time" and "Newsweek," current copies are available for circulation.

## THE LIBRARY LOCATION

The designation of a room to house the library was the next major step. An area of approximately 1000 square feet was deemed adequate to accommodate a potential clientele of 300 or more, to properly house the collection, and to provide an adequate base from which library services would be extended to the entire company. Not all of Riley's technical literature could be gathered in this one room, nor was it meant to be. Certain collections would still be maintained in the various departments.

After consideration of the areas offered by Riley, it was decided that the old Service Department, then used by our Japanese licensee, was an ideal space for the library. Its 800 square feet was centrally located to most of its potential users. It had the advantage over the other areas in the building for being a discrete space, not continuous with offices and therefore more quiet; the elongated shape with a single entrance at one end expedited the

FIGURE 1.

restriction of any unauthorized traffic of materials; and there was sufficient natural lighting to make a pleasant study area in such a way that valuable wall space was not wasted on large windows. Certain improvements were needed. The room had a cave-like appearance, well-worn linoleum, old paint over brick, and a mass of exposed wiring and pipes. Approximate figures for reconstruction are given:

| | |
|---|---|
| Carpeting: 119 sq. yds. × $12/yd.<br>$1,428 installed | (allow)$ 1,500 |
| Front Wall: Reworked to include a door and lock<br>extended to ceiling | 1,800 |
| Walls: Framing and board panelling @ $5,000 &<br>duct work @ $1,000 | 6,000 |
| Ceiling: Suspended ceiling 1060 sq. ft. × $1 + /ft. =<br>$1,100 plus sprinklers, lighting & electrical | 6,100 |
| Total: | $15,400 |

While reconstruction was in progress, the librarian was given an office in the Fuel Burning Department where she accumulated technical literature, weeded through collections, and designed a floor plan. It was at this point that the company decided more space was needed for the Quality Assurance Department, choosing the front half of the library; thus reducing our space to approximately 400 square feet.


## LIBRARY SPACE PLANNING: FURNITURE & EQUIPMENT


Due to the reduction in space, a new floor plan was designed to allow maximum use of the area now allotted. Items were purchased with this in mind; utilizing every square foot to its best advantage. A list of major furnishings and equipment is given:

| | | |
|---|---|---|
| 84″ Steel Library Shelving | 23 @ 106.70/ea | $ 2,454.10 |
| Woodgrain Dictionary Stand | 1 @ 125.25/ea | 125.25 |
| Double End Panels (2 pair) | 4 @ 62.50/ea | 250.00 |
| Sloping Shelves | 30 @ 15.00/ea | 450.00 |
| Double Reference Shelves | 2 @ 39.50/ea | 79.00 |
| Book Supports | 100 @ 2.27/ea | 227.00 |
| 5 Drawer Lateral Files | 7 @ 535.00/ea | 3,745.00 |

| Woodgrain Desks | 2 @ 341.50/ea | 683.00 |
| Woodgrain Tables 30″ × 60″ | 5 @ 183.10/ea | 915.50 |
| Microfiche Readers | 2 @ 250.00/ea | 500.00 |
| Chairs | 11 @ 88.00/ea | 968.00 |
| Newspaper Rack | 1 @ 62.00/ea | 62.00 |
| Book Truck | 1 @ 72.00/ea | 72.00 |
| Total = | | $10,530.85 |

Equipment such as typewriters and clocks were extras owned by the company. Artwork was donated by a semi-professional photographer in the Advertising Department. Slightly over a year, after much preparation, the library was opened for business. (See Figure 2.)

The present library layout is the originally designed plan. Note space and time saving techniques. The reference section is located directly behind the librarian's desk for quick and ready reference phone calls. Above her desk are double shelves storing everyday material; LC Schedules, DIALOG Files, *Books in Print*, etc. Tables are arranged in a continuous grouping and the newspaper rack is wall mounted as opposed to a floor model. Due to the space restriction, newspapers are kept for one week only and our collection of 123 periodicals is housed for three years. A requisition has been submitted in the 1983 budget proposal for a reader/printer to alleviate this problem. ASME papers, patents, and other technical literature are stored in the lateral files along with Riley reports. DOE, EPA, and EPRI reports as well as a major part of our collection of approximately 1200 books, reports, and technical papers are shelved in the 84″ units in a section separate from the books. The assistant's desk is located adjacent to another set of lateral files for simple retrieval of office supplies.

The system most unique to the library is our online cataloging system; not to be confused with OCLC cataloging. Using a Digital Decscope we are able to eliminate the standard card catalog, card reproduction, typing, and filing, thus saving space, time and money. All data entered into the computer is transmitted into a Digital VAX 11/780 central computer in the Technical Service Department. The librarian must submit a request to Computer Operations when an updated report is desired. The request must specify either a printed or microfiche copy. The entire series of reports are run each time. Selective or partial reports are not possible. Due to this system, our entire card catalog is on microfiche, stored in a simple slotted binder. Printed reports formatted on 11″ × 15″

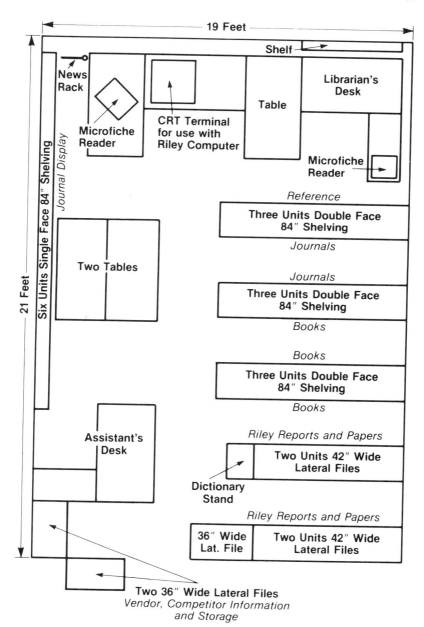

## PRESENT LIBRARY LAYOUT

FIGURE 2.

computer paper can be used for editing, although the system does have online editing capabilities. Microfiche is updated about every three months. Recent acquisitions can be accessed directly through the computer.

## SUMMARY

The area and layout have worked well in the library's four year history. More recently we have felt the need for additional space. If a reader/printer is approved, it would open up two shelving units for expansion. Another recent development is the relocation of the Quality Assurance Department. Since their move, the original front half of the library is now unoccupied. We are hopeful that this area will be approved for library expansion. If so, additional shelving and lateral files will be purchased along with the hope of obtaining our own computer terminal for online literature searching directly in the library. Office space will be provided with plans for a small reading room along with tables, chairs, a separate microfiche catalog and reader.

Presently, regular weeding is necessary in order to maintain room for our collection. The addition of one more range of shelving, which would fit in our present space, would carry us at least another year. Because of the tight quarters, the outlook for additional space approval is good.

# Creating New Library Facilities for the Bendix Advanced Technology Center

Ted Rupprecht

**ABSTRACT.** The new Bendix Advanced Technology Center Library was formed by selecting a core collection from the older Research Laboratories' Library in Michigan and moving it to the new research center in Maryland. The author describes the relocation of the new collection and the re-establishment of a library system serving fifty scientists. Bibliographic control of both the collections was maintained throughout the move.

## INTRODUCTION

The Bendix Research Laboratories (BRL) were established in Detroit in 1948. By 1952 the Laboratories had moved to a new building in suburban Southfield, Michigan. A library was established at that time utilizing 1,000 square feet of office space. After ten years, the collection consisted of 5,000 technical reports and 8,000 books and journals.

The author was employed as Librarian in 1962 to supervise two non-professionals. During the next few years, service was improved by augmenting the inadequate collection with improved interlibrary loan procedures. American Library Association cataloging standards were introduced and in-depth cataloging of internal technical reports initiated. By the early 1970s the Library operated on a budget. Reading space was improved and in 1974 online searching began in *Dialog, Orbit* and the *New York Times Information Bank*. The first all-Bendix Library Conference was also held in 1974.

During most of the 1970s, the staff consisted of two professionals and two paraprofessionals. Growth and improvement, of

Ted Rupprecht is Supervisor, Library Services, Bendix Advanced Technology Center, 9140 Old Annapolis Road, Columbia, MD 21045. He has the BLS and MLS degrees from the University of Illinois.

course, were not constant, but by the end of the decade the Library had a collection of some 15,000 books and journals, a union catalog on technical topics with nearby Lawrence Institute of Technology, automated routing of journals and a Keyword-in-Context (KWIC) index to thousands of society papers.

## WHY A NEW LIBRARY?

Beginning in 1978, Bendix began to review and rethink its scientific and technical capabilities. Bendix, along with other corporations, found itself reducing levels of funding for research and development during times of economic stress. These trends forced the Research Laboratories to serve only the short-term research needs of corporate divisions while long-range projects were increasingly strung out during funding declines.

In December, 1979, a corporate decision was made to establish an Advanced Technology Center (ATC) in order to assure long-term research. The Research Laboratories were renamed and replaced by the Engineering Development Center (EDC). Both ATC and EDC were under the direction of John J. Martin, Vice President and General Manager. ATC was assigned longer-term research and exploratory development while EDC was assigned advanced development, testing, evaluation and an assistance role in Division engineering and manufacturing. The Library remained in EDC and served the technical staffs of both entities. To facilitate concentration and develop esprit de corps, ATC staff members (a cadre drawn initially from the Research Laboratories staff) were moved to a nearby office building. ATC's assignments were to determine new "thrust areas" for long-range corporate research and to select a new site for the permanent location of the new Advanced Technology Center.

It was easy to see that this newly-formed group of scientists with well-defined projects, top-management support and plans for an eventual move to a new laboratory would soon be in need of its own library service. The purpose of this paper is to describe the initial interaction with management, the nature of the user groups and the planning methods used to select a core collection of materials for a library service that was to be moved from one state to another.

## THE USER COMMUNITY

By late 1980, the ATC Site Selection Committee had chosen Columbia, Maryland, as the site for the new laboratory. Continuing their work on their thrust areas in another building, the ATC staff members, along with EDC users now made up two separate user groups who were both dependent on the old Research Laboratories Library.

The ATC group, although half the size of the EDC group, was by far the more difficult to serve because of its high demand for complex information. A simple tabulation of major library activity for the two groups shows this difference. (See Table 1.)

In general, the ATC user groups could be characterized as high-frequency users of scientific journals, technical reports, society papers, books and conference proceedings in narrow subject areas. The Research Laboratories Library had provided a 233% increase in interlibrary loan service over an eight-year period accompanied by a 50% increase in book acquisition. Library users were accustomed to accurate and timely retrieval with prompt dissemination.

To keep nomenclature simple, the EDC or donor Library, will be referred to as the Southfield Library and the recipient library as the ATC Library. By January of 1981, the ATC technical staff had grown to about forty members consisting of twenty-four PhD's, thirteen with MS degrees and three with BS degrees. Their backgrounds were in physics, mechanical engineering, electronics and chemistry.

### TABLE I

#### 1980 Activity of ATC and EDC

|                    | ATC  | EDC  | TOTAL |
|--------------------|------|------|-------|
| Interlibrary loans | 63%  | 37%  | 100%  |
| Acquisitions       | 64.8 | 35.2 | 100   |
| Literature Searches| 54.2 | 45.8 | 100   |

## FIRST STEPS

In late 1980, sensing that few decisions had been made by ATC management concerning library service, the Library staff initiated an informal meeting with the Associate Director of Research to explore a set of assumptions thought to be relevant to ATC library service at the new site. The exchange of views on the assumptions served to focus management's attention on the information problems as viewed by the two professional librarians and in turn, to inform the librarians of management's schedules, priorities and procedures. The final assumptions which resulted were that:

1. ATC would become the research center in Bendix most closely associated with "basic research."
2. ATC population could grow during the next two-to-four years to about 150 scientists with supporting staff.
3. ATC would gradually move to Columbia over a period of months.
4. As each ATC segment moved to Columbia, it would need a flow of information up until the time of the move and immediately upon "start up" at the new site.
5. Each segment would expect information services to remain at the present level of professionalism during the moves in (4).
6. The ATC staff's need for information would veer from its present position in applied science to the more basic and theoretical. This new material would form a new Scientific Information Center or Library.
7. Cataloged materials (books, proceedings, society papers and government reports) charged to ATC staff in Southfield would be moved only if appropriate changes were made in the card catalogs. (To do otherwise would be to destroy an important index at Southfield and to create informational havoc at the new site.)

The resulting discussion revealed that ATC's mission would be to perform primarily basic research, that the staff of scientists would steadily increase and that in six months staff, projects and equipment would begin moving to Columbia. Continuous library service would be needed. A new Library was in the plans for

Columbia—space was already allocated and a professional would be in charge. All cataloged materials moved to Columbia would be removed in a manner that would allow functioning collections in both Southfield and Columbia.

Recommendations were made in the following areas:

1. The Associate Director would appoint an ad hoc Library Committee to serve as advisors in collection development.
2. The Library Staff would start work immediately to select new subscriptions and to divert current subscriptions to Columbia.
3. The ATC staff would pack those books charged to them when they moved. An extra month would be allowed to select additional books.

The informal meeting ended with a description of library resources available to the members of the ATC staff in the Washington/Baltimore corridor. Union lists and library directories from the area were used to point out differences likely to be experienced by ATC scientists in a new library milieu.

At the end of the meeting, a sense of direction had been established and fundamental concepts aired. The Library staff could plan realistically for the division of the collection along user-community lines. The creation of a new library from a donor, the maintenance of bibliographic integrity in both collections and the physical removal of one collection to another state suddenly seemed overwhelming. It was time to "think through" and to organize.

## *CHARTING THE EVENTS*

A simple tool was used to sort things out. First, every possible action related to separation, continuance, transfer and re-establishment of library service was recorded—one action at a time, on separate cards. A couple of days were spent on this. Then the cards were shuffled in probable sequence from the first action to the last. From this a task/time chart—tasks on one axis, time to complete them on the other—was formed. This chart is sometimes known as a Gantt[1] Chart from H.L. Gantt, its originator. Our use of this chart is shown in Figure 1.

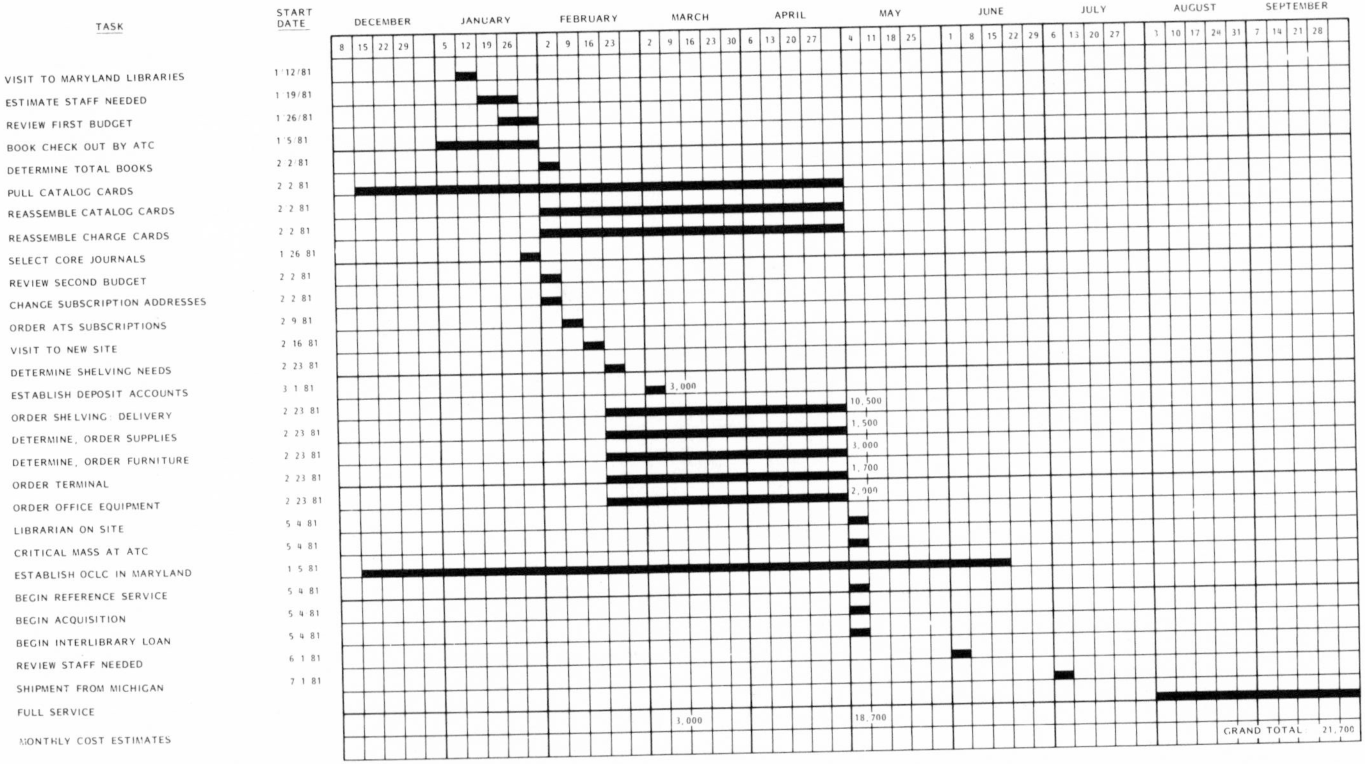

| TASK | START DATE |
|---|---|
| VISIT TO MARYLAND LIBRARIES | 1 12 81 |
| ESTIMATE STAFF NEEDED | 1 19 81 |
| REVIEW FIRST BUDGET | 1 26 81 |
| BOOK CHECK OUT BY ATC | 1 5 81 |
| DETERMINE TOTAL BOOKS | 2 2 81 |
| PULL CATALOG CARDS | 2 2 81 |
| REASSEMBLE CATALOG CARDS | 2 2 81 |
| REASSEMBLE CHARGE CARDS | 2 2 81 |
| SELECT CORE JOURNALS | 1 26 81 |
| REVIEW SECOND BUDGET | 2 2 81 |
| CHANGE SUBSCRIPTION ADDRESSES | 2 2 81 |
| ORDER ATS SUBSCRIPTIONS | 2 9 81 |
| VISIT TO NEW SITE | 2 16 81 |
| DETERMINE SHELVING NEEDS | 2 23 81 |
| ESTABLISH DEPOSIT ACCOUNTS | 3 1 81 |
| ORDER SHELVING, DELIVERY | 2 23 81 |
| DETERMINE, ORDER SUPPLIES | 2 23 81 |
| DETERMINE, ORDER FURNITURE | 2 23 81 |
| ORDER TERMINAL | 2 23 81 |
| ORDER OFFICE EQUIPMENT | 2 23 81 |
| LIBRARIAN ON SITE | 5 4 81 |
| CRITICAL MASS AT ATC | 5 4 81 |
| ESTABLISH OCLC IN MARYLAND | 1 5 81 |
| BEGIN REFERENCE SERVICE | 5 4 81 |
| BEGIN ACQUISITION | 5 4 81 |
| BEGIN INTERLIBRARY LOAN | 5 4 81 |
| REVIEW STAFF NEEDED | 6 1 81 |
| SHIPMENT FROM MICHIGAN | 7 1 81 |
| FULL SERVICE | |
| MONTHLY COST ESTIMATES | |

Timeline columns: DECEMBER (8, 15, 22, 29); JANUARY (5, 12, 19, 26); FEBRUARY (2, 9, 16, 23); MARCH (2, 9, 16, 23, 30); APRIL (6, 13, 20, 27); MAY (4, 11, 18, 25); JUNE (1, 8, 15, 22, 29); JULY (6, 13, 20, 27); AUGUST (3, 10, 17, 24, 31); SEPTEMBER (7, 14, 21, 28)

Cost figures noted on chart: 3,000; 10,500; 1,500; 3,000; 1,700; 2,700; 18,700; 1,000

GRAND TOTAL 21,700

Figure 1. Establishing the ATC Library - Selected Tasks

The purpose of the chart was to serve as a starting point for planning, a guide for placing orders and a reminder of deadlines. By reading down the list, a self-explanatory sequence of events is evident. The first step was obviously circumspect—who were the librarians in the neighborhood? How far away, and is there inter-action? How does location influence staff?

In mid-point, the action consists mostly of decisions on quantities and the placing of orders. The lower quarter of the list shows the new library in place and the beginning of on-site service.

The chart was useful in several other ways. First, it helped inform management, unfamiliar with internal library administration, of the necessity for certain sequential actions and the need for employing part-time staff at peak loads. Secondly, it was an effective tool for approximating costs. A cost-estimate is visible at the end of the time strips in March and May. Monthly cost-estimates were easily translated by the Accounting department into capitalization and expense accounts. "Peaks" or "loads" could be predicted. During meetings, supporting amounts in the monthly totals and "time strips" were instantly available for explaining totals. This eliminated larger presentation charts and kept the whole operation desk-size.

Lastly, the most obvious benefit of the chart was its use in planning the spread of the work load. By reading downward in any month, the planner can spot "black areas" containing an overload of the system. When this occurs, it is necessary to rearrange the starting dates.

Charting in this manner forces the planner to exercise judgement on when to start an event, to estimate how long it will take and how much it will cost. The primary value of the chart is in its construction. When completed, it serves mainly as a guide and the individual user can decide whether or not to record the actual completion dates. It was helpful in some of the busiest weeks to lift some of the dates and projects from the major chart and create a more detailed second chart—fine tuning, in effect. This second chart was useful for tracking some of the deadlines applied to other staff members, getting answers from mangement on invoicing and accounting procedures at the new location, hiring dates for temporary help and establishing frequent vendor contacts. Both for an overview and for close work, charting events was an absolute necessity.

## ASSEMBLING THE CORE COLLECTIONS

In dividing the collections we were faced with two requirements: first, to leave behind a working collection in the Southfield Library under the Cataloging and Reference Librarian; second, to extract a collection capable of serving the major start-up needs of the new Advanced Technology Center under the supervision of the author. We were generally agreed that the donor collection should be approximately divided so that the theoretical and scientific publications would go to ATC and that the engineering and applied technology books and trade journals would stay with the Southfield Library. As any special librarian knows, only rough delineations can be drawn in these circumstances and in our case our precepts were frequently overthrown because of the type of project that could be found in either group.

### Books

Earlier, we had established with the Associate Director of Research that a core collection of books would be formed by releasing the Southfield Library books charged to ATC and by allowing the ATC staff members to enlarge their holdings by a month-long selection period from the stacks. Library policy over the years had been to keep a record by surname of outstanding loans, so it was a simple process to begin pulling the shelf list and card-sets, working from the surname lists.

Figure 1 will show that January was the "free selection" period for ATC and that during the week of February 2 we were determining the universe of books in the new collection. Once determined, we requested that ATC stop checking out books so that the new collection would not grow. We needed a finite number of books to work with.

Under these plans, we made photocopies of each shelf list and main entry on 8½-by-11-inch sheets. These were filed in their respective orders in loose-leaf notebooks. In this way the Southfield Library was never without a main entry and the shelf-list order of the card-sets gave constant access to holdings records. After the completion of the new ATC catalog, the Southfield Library had a complete loose-leaf record of the main entries "missing" from its collection along with a picture of the shelf-list to correct the inevitable copy and volume number anomalies.

Although the chart shows we planned to reassemble a new catalog as we pulled cards, this soon proved impractical because of our small staff. A graduate librarian was employed temporarily from April through June. Her work resulted in a new catalog with cataloging and copy-number errors corrected as well as a complete set of tailor-made filing rules. The evolution of the new catalog is too detailed to treat here, but the author will be pleased to discuss it in correspondence with interested readers.

## *Journals*

In establishing journal service, we needed to maintain continuity in both Southfield and Columbia for titles common to both and to start a complete annual list of unique 1981 titles for the ATC Library. This was complicated by the fact that no ATC Library staff was scheduled to be on-site for check-in until after June 1. We were fortunate, though, in that we were working early in the calendar year and could place full-year orders with most publishers up until April 1.

The list and holdings of the 500 titles at Southfield had been entered in a menu-program in a VAX computer a couple of years earlier. To help resolve the problems of continuous journal service, four categories were established, each one representing an action that solved one of the four problems that was peculiar to transferring journal service from the Southfield Library to ATC Columbia.

Each category was identified by a code in which the first three letters—ATC—were common. The entire Southfield list was edited by assigning ATC codes to those titles going to Columbia. We next asked for a print-out of the "ATC" items and received a special ATC periodical list with each title bearing one of the four categories. The final edited ATC list is shown in Figure 2. The categories used were:

—(ATC 2nd) A duplicate subscription, ordered for the year 1981 to be delivered to Southfield and stored there and moved to Columbia when the facilities were ready after June 1.
—(ATC E-Div) Certain subscriptions received in Southfield but reassigned to ATC and diverted from the Southfield address to the Columbia address effective June 1.

(ATC 2ND) = SECOND COPY ON ORDER
(ATC E-DIV) = DIVERTED FROM SOUTHFIELD SUB LIST TO ATC COLUMBIA
(ATC HLDGS) = BOUND AND UNBOUND RUNS GOING TO COLUMBIA
(ATC NEW) = NEW SUSCRIPTION FOR ATC.

| TITLE | YEARS | B | DI | DL | EI | EL | F | P |
|---|---|---|---|---|---|---|---|---|
| ACOUSTICAL SOCIETY OF AMERICA (ATC HLDGS) | 1960- | B | | | | EL | | P |
| AMERICAN MATHEMATICAL MONTHLY (ATC HLDGS) | 1977- | | | | | EL | | P |
| AMERICAN SOCIETY FOR INFORMATION SCIENCE (ATC HLDGS) | 1979- | | | | | | F | P |
| AMERICAN SOC. FOR INFORMATION SCIENCE (ATC HLDGS) | 1977- | | | | | | F | P |
| APPLIED MATHEMATICAL MODELLING (ATC HLDGS) | 1978- | | | | | EL | | |
| APPLIED OPTICS (ATC HLDGS) | 1962- | B | | DL | | EL | | P |
| APPLIED PHYSICS LETTERS (ATC HLDGS) | 1962- | B | | DL | | | | P |
| APPLIED SPECTROSCOPY (ATC HLDGS) | 1958- | | | | | | | P |
| AVIATION WEEK AND SPACE TECHNOLOGY (ATC E-DIV) | CURRENT + 3 | | | | | EL | | |
| AVIATION WEEK ANS SPACE TECHNOLOGY (ATC E-DIV) | CURRENT + 3 | | | | | EL | | |
| BULLETIN OF ALLOY PHASE DIAGRAMS (ATC 2ND) | 1981- | | | | | EL | | |
| BUSINESS WEEK (ATC E-DIV) | 1981- | | | | | EL | | |
| BUSINESS WEEK (ATC E-DIV) | 1981- | | | | | EL | | |
| CARBON (ATC HLDGS) | 1963- | B | | | | EL | | P |
| CARBON (ATC E-DIV) | 1981- | | | | | EL | | |
| CHEMICAL AND ENGINEERING NEWS (ATC 2ND) | 1981- | | | | | EL | | |
| CHEMICAL ENGINEERING (ATC 2ND) | 1981- | | | | | EL | | |
| CHEMICAL WEEK (ATC 2ND) | 1976 | | | | | EL | | |
| COMMUNICATIONS ON PHYSICS (ATC HLDGS) | 1981- | | | | | EL | | P |
| COMPOSITES (ATC 2ND) | CURRENT + 3 | | | | | EL | F | P |
| ELECTRO-OPTICAL SYSTEMS DESIGN (ATC HLDGS) | 1981 | | | | | EL | | |
| ELECTRONIC NEWS (ATC E-DIV) | 1981 | | | | | EL | | |
| ELECTRONICS (ATC E-DIV) | 1981- | | | | | EL | | |
| ELECTRONICS (ATC E-DIV) | 1979- | | | | EI | | | |
| FEN (FINITE ELEMENT NEWS) (ATC E-DIV) | JUNE, 1981- | | | | | | | P |
| FORTUNE (ATC 2ND) | 1974- | B | | | | | F | P |
| GOLD BULLETIN (ATC HLDGS) | 1981- | | | DL | | EL | | |
| HARVARD BUSINESS REVIEW (ATC 2ND) | 1981 (?) | B | | | | EL | | |
| INDUSTRIAL RESEARCH/DEVELOPMENT (ATC 2ND) | 1961-79 | B | | | | | | |
| INFRARED PHYSICS (ATC HLDGS) | 1969-72 | | | | | EL | | P |
| INNOVATION (ATC HLDGS) | 1979- | | | | | EL | | |
| INTERNATIONAL JOURNAL FOR NUMERICAL METHODS IN ENGINEERING (ATC HLDGS) | 1973-79 | | | | | EL | | P |
| INTERNATIONAL JOURNAL OF CHEMICAL KINETICS (ATC HLDGS) | 1971-79 | | | | | EL | | P |
| INTERNATIONAL JOURNAL OF MASS SPECTROMETRY AND ION PHYSICS (ATC HLDGS) | 1971- | | | | | EL | | P |
| INTERNATIONAL JOURNAL OF POWDER METALLURGY & POWDER TECHNOLOGY (ATC HLDGS) | 1968-79 | B | | | | EL | | P |
| JAPANESE JOURNAL OF APPLIED PHYSICS (ATC HLDGS) | 1947- | B | | | | EL | | P |
| JOURNAL OF APPLIED PHYSICS (ATC 2ND) | 1981- | | | DL | | EL | | P |
| JOURNAL OF COMPOSITE MATERIALS (ATC HLDGS) | 1979- | | | | | EL | | P |
| JOURNAL OF COMPOSITE MATERIALS (ATC 2ND) | 1981- | | | | | EL | | P |
| JOURNAL OF COMPOSITE MATERIALS (ATC HLDGS) | 1969-74, 81- | | | | | | | P |
| JOURNAL OF CRYSTAL GROWTH (ATC HLDGS) (ATC NEW) | 1977-79 | | | | | EL | | P |
| JOURNAL OF DESIGN AUTOMATION AND FAULT-TOLERANT COMPUTING (ATC HLDGS) | 1977- | | | | | EL | | P |
| JOURNAL OF ENERGY (ATC DIV-E) (ATC HLDGS) | 1978- | | | | | | | P |
| JOURNAL OF GUIDANCE AND CONTROL (ATC HLDGS) (ATC E-DIV) | 1968- | | | DL | | EL | | P |
| JOURNAL OF PHYSICS A (ATC HLDGS) | 1968- | | | | | EL | | P |

Figure 2. ATC Library Journals Selected by Category

—(ATC New) A new subscription to a new title handled by Southfield as (ATC 2nd).

—(ATC Holdings) Holdings, bound and unbound, as shown in the "years" column to be moved to Columbia.

The list as shown in Figure 2 was used to determine subject coverage in consultation with the ad hoc Library Committee. The (ATC E-Div) list was printed separately and sent to our subscription agency who arranged for the address changes from Southfield to Columbia. The (ATC New) list was also sent to the agency for new subscriptions to unique titles.

We used the (ATC Holdings) list to pack bound and unbound journals in sixteen-by-ten-by-twelve-inch boxes known as "record cartons" in commercial moving. These were readily available, stackable, had a good closure and the proper burst-strength. A good discussion of cartons and moving containers is available in Spyers-Duran.[2]

Each box was serially numbered beginning with number one in the A's. About forty boxes (or approximately fifty linear feet) fit on a skid or common shipping pallet, measuring forty-by-forty-eight inches. Close supervision is necessary to see that the pallets are loaded so that the highest numbers are loaded first and the lowest numbers last (on top), and that each pallet is numbered in series. Keeping the pallets in order and loading them on the mover's truck so that the lowest numbers are the "first out" will give a continuous alphabetic flow from truck to stack.

## Reference Collection

The Library staff developed a reference collection based mainly on duplications of the most-used works associated with the ATC staff. Complete acquisition, cataloging and processing support for the reference and circulating collection was supplied to the ATC Library from January to September 1981. By the September 22, 1981, Open House for the new facility, a core collection of journals was on the shelf, the catalog in place and fully-cataloged reference books were "on-stream" from the Southfield Library. The ATC Library staff now consisted of the author as Librarian and one Library Technician serving some 50 members of the technical staff.

## SPACE

The laboratory building chosen as the site for the Advanced Technology Center is located in rolling farmland on the northern boundary of Columbia, Maryland, about fifteen miles south of Baltimore and thirty-five north of Washington. In February 1981 the author made his first visit to the new site in order to view the space assigned to the Library. The proposed area was well-situated on the main floor of the building near offices and laboratories. The floor area was a rectangle, twenty-seven by fifty-three feet, enclosing 1,431 square feet. It was in use by the lessee of the building as a document storage and microfilm processing area and did not become available to Bendix until July.

During this first visit, and with the assistance of the local representative of the shelving manufacturer, careful measurements were made of actual wall length, column projections and variances in ceiling height. There were no windows. After a layout was drawn up in Southfield, the shelving order was placed and delivery and loading of the stacks took place in September 1981. All of the wall space except one corner used as the staff work area was lined with single-face shelving. Expansion was planned to be moved into double-face, free-standing stacks placed across the narrow dimension of the room.

### Recombination

Almost exactly one year after Open House in Columbia, the entire technical portion of the Southfield Library journal and reference collections suddenly became available to the ATC Library. The Southfield Library staff had been reassigned to maintain marketing, financial, general business and management information at corporate headquarters. The remaining technical staff at EDC had also been reassigned, thus making available long runs of applied technology periodicals and technical society journals. In response, ATC management requested that the author draw new floor plans to absorb this additional material. The new plan called for the removal of a wall and the incorporation of the hall behind it into the Library's floor area.

Removing this wall extended the floor area up to a glass wall fifty-three feet long overlooking the building's inner courtyard and fountains—a delightful improvement in the light level and ambiance of the room. The total floor space was increased from 1431 to 1749 square feet and shelving from 500 to 1458 linear feet. About 610 linear feet, or a 37.7% increase in library materials, were to be shipped from Southfield.

The southern half of the room was planned as a stack area and in the northern half all of the furniture is removable. This permits the conversion of some 1100 square feet of library space to a folding-chair auditorium that can seat approximately 130. Work was completed on this renovation on October 29, 1982, and the new floor plan is presented in Figure 3. A photograph of the reader/study area is shown in Figure 4.

The west end of the room is nearest the front of the building and user in-flow is heaviest here. The door in the east wall is used for deliveries and gives user-access to the copier just outside the door. The rest of the room is a conventional separation of the work-area from the reader/study area with the latter located near the circulation desk and card catalog.

The stacks in ranges A through F are double-face, nine feet long and flanked on each side by two single-face sections mounted on rolling carriages that run on aluminum-alloy tracks laid on carpeting. A guide-rail at the top securely holds the rolling single-face sections upright. This shelving arrangement provides a 20% increase (from 864 to 1080 linear feet) over eight conventional double face ranges spaced with the same aisle-width in the same floor area. The carriages and the tracks are manufactured as a system by DENSTOR Division of Anderson and Associates, Inc., 24333 Indoplex Circle, Farmington, Michigan, 48018, and are adaptable to most standard library shelving. We find that there is no user resistance. On the contrary, users are intrigued with the space-saving features and very quickly adapt to the system.

The OCLC terminal, the portable terminal and the microfiche reader form an experimental cluster that allows the Librarian to move easily from task to task. This portion of the layout is subject to rearrangement as experience dictates. The tables, for instance, waste space and will be replaced with computer furniture when feasible, while the counter-height book shelves provide a new and convenient work surface. When conversion of the Library to an auditorium is no longer necessary, stacks can be lengthened northward if necessary.

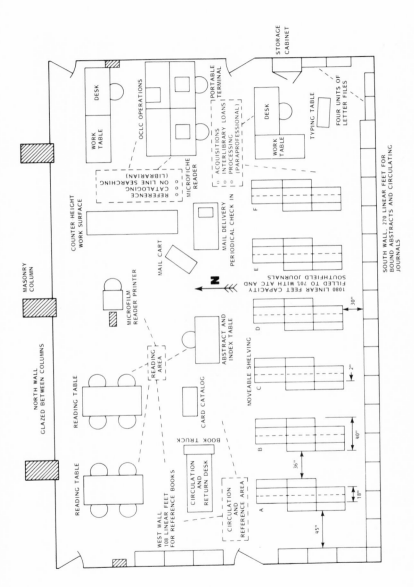

Figure 3. Floor Plan for the ATC Library, November 1, 1982

FIGURE 4.

## *EVALUATION*

Its "mitosis" complete, the ATC Library has also just completed its first year of independent operation. Essentially, the move can be considered a successful transfer of materials and service standards. No new functions were planned, but organized information and reference support to the members of the technical staff were continuously provided.

Support from the staff at the Southfield Library (mainly in acquisitions and cataloging), along with the special hospitality of the neighboring Gibson Library at Johns Hopkins Applied Physics Laboratory, made the transition easier. In 1983, the ATC Library's major concern will be staff development.

During 1981-82, limitations of the core collection soon became evident and early in 1982 a Library Advisory Board (LAB) of working scientists was formed to meet with the Librarian on plans for collection enrichment. Recent acquisition of the technical holdings from Southfield will substantially alter the work of the LAB which had just begun to investigate the role of microforms at ATC. This year the Librarian requested an advisory session with the LAB on renewing the subscription list.

The new catalog functions as intended. It was used at an increasing rate as projects and books arrived from Southfield. Allowing each member of the technical staff to move his books with his office or laboratory worked well. Over the months there has been a slow "trickle-back" as these books are replaced with newer ones purchased for new tasks. All library materials were delivered undamaged and in sequence.

## *CONCLUSIONS*

This experience showed that both the planner and his schedule must be flexible. Delays in the availability of space at the target location, unforseen problems in production or delays because of seasonal back-logs could cause upsets. It was found to be important to try to get an early start placing orders to be ready to change emphasis as the plan unfolds.

Activities that librarians do well—identifying, listing, sorting and scheduling—all worked smoothly. Areas outside a librarian's normal ken, such as negotiating delivery dates and shipping terms, were found to be best left to the experts in the purchasing and shipping departments. It is best to ask their advice and then plan a scheduled follow-up.

First-time library movers will find little specific help in the literature because libraries differ widely and so do the circumstances of their moves. These first-timers should review the literature and then seek the advice of someone who has successfully carried out a move and who is still willing to talk about it.

## REFERENCES

1. Clark, Wallace. *The Gantt chart; a working tool of management.* 2d ed. London: Pitman; 1942. 158 p.

2. Spyers-Duran, Peter. *Moving library materials.* Rev. ed. Chicago: American Library Association; 1965.

# Facilities for Northwestern University's Science-Engineering Library

## Janet Ayers

**ABSTRACT.** Consolidation of several branch sci-tech libraries at Northwestern University provides a more efficient operation and improves user services. This paper describes one example of a successful merger of three libraries to form a computerized multidisciplinary unit.

The Seeley G. Mudd Library for Science and Engineering at Northwestern University, Evanston, Illinois, incorporates the collections from three former branches: Astronomy, Biology, and the Technological Institute Libraries. The Library is a three story limestone clad window wall building with a net area of approximately 55 thousand square feet. It is the largest branch library on the Evanston campus; two smaller collections, Geology and Mathematics, remain in the respective subject buildings.

Located on a landfill area on the Lake Michigan shore, the Library is directly east of the spacious Technological Institute. The latter building houses lecture rooms, offices, and laboratories for seven engineering departments, the Departments of Physics and Chemistry, and two interdisciplinary research centers. A glass enclosed walkway leads from the Technological Institute directly into the Science-Engineering Library. The Hogan Biological Sciences Building is located conveniently within 200 feet of the Library.

## BACKGROUND AND PLANNING

When three former science branch libraries became acutely overcrowded a decade ago, there was no way to remodel or to expand

Janet Ayers has a BS in Chemistry from Northwestern University and the MS in Library Science from Simmons College. She is presently the Physical Sciences and Engineering Librarian at the Seeley G. Mudd Library. Northwestern University, Evanston, IL 60201.

any of the existing facilities. Fortunately Northwestern did not possess a tradition of numerous branch libraries scattered in separate buildings. Therefore, the individual collections did not have to remain intact and the three libraries could be merged.

The Library Planning Committee met frequently over several years. Both faculty and library administration were actively involved in the planning and decisions. The Committee stressed the interdisciplinary nature of the sciences and specified further that the new library structure should possess: a flexible, open plan making it adaptable to future needs; a conveniently located microform area with adequate equipment and storage; and a provision for computerized services, including public terminals.

Once the cornerstone was laid in November 1976 construction was rapid and the building was completed ahead of schedule. When the Library opened in July 1977 the collection numbered 170,000 volumes, with the combined capacity of the first and third floor stacks deliberately set at 200,000 volumes.

From the time of initial planning it was expected that a major part of the collection, the older and lesser used material, would be stored off-site. Thus in 1977 the new Library's stacks contained 90,000 volumes; the remaining 80,000 were in storage at the main University Library. The decision for major off-site storage has worked well. Requests for stored material are serviced on a daily basis, Monday through Friday.

## SPECIAL FEATURES

### Arrangement

The central entrances and exits are on the second floor. All Library services and offices also are concentrated on this level. The second floor includes circulation services, reserve book stacks, reference material, abstract and index section, card catalogs, public terminals, a faculty reading room, library conference room, and a microform area. Over 1735 currently received periodical titles are displayed on special sloping shelves. (Figures 1 & 2.)

Level three contains: bound periodicals arranged in call number order; a group study room; a dual purpose group study/volume sorting room; and photocopy facilities. On level one all non-periodicals are shelved. In addition to a shelving/study room and a

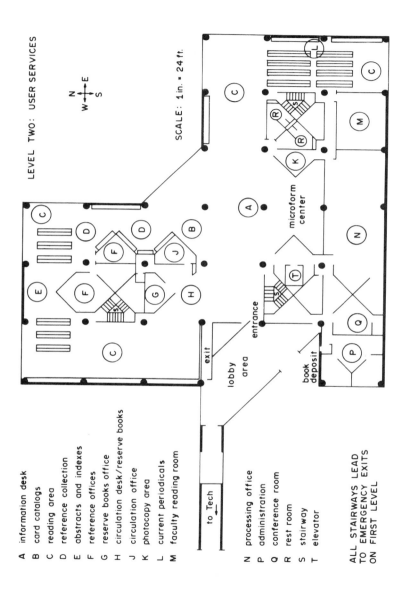

LEVEL TWO: USER SERVICES

N
W—E
S

SCALE: 1 in. = 24 ft.

A  information desk
B  card catalogs
C  reading area
D  reference collection
E  abstracts and indexes
F  reference offices
G  reserve books office
H  circulation desk/reserve books
J  circulation office
K  photocopy area
L  current periodicals
M  faculty reading room

N  processing office
P  administration
Q  conference room
R  rest room
S  stairway
T  elevator

ALL STAIRWAYS LEAD
TO EMERGENCY EXITS
ON FIRST LEVEL

SEELEY G. MUDD LIBRARY, NORTHWESTERN UNIVERSITY

FIGURE 1.

79

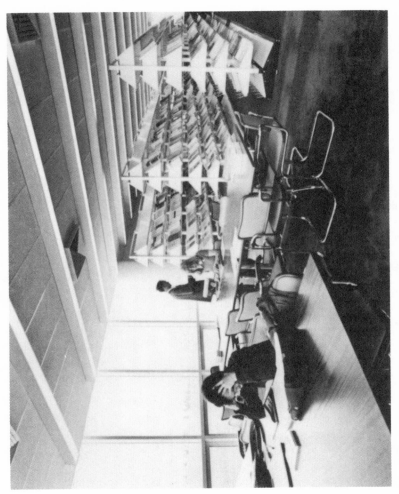

FIGURE 2.

photocopy machine, there is a loading dock, a machine room, and a staff lounge equipped with sink, stove, and refrigerator.

The general arrangement is such that users either go up one floor from the second (main)level to find bound periodicals or they go down to the first floor to locate monographs and monographic series.

## *Hours and Staffing*

During the school year the Library operates until midnight seven days a week and is open a total of 5500 hours annually. After 5 p.m. on weekdays and all day Saturday and Sunday, student staffing is used. A minimum of two persons must be on duty when the Library is open.

The eleven full time positions include four professional librarians and seven staff members. The Head Librarian is assisted by a Life Sciences Librarian, a Physical Sciences and Engineering Librarian, and a Technical Services Librarian. Forty students, the majority on work-study, are employed part-time during the regular school term.

## *Computerization*

Northwestern University Library's computerized system began in 1970, when the three-tower main library was opened. The *N*orthwestern *O*nline *T*otal *I*ntegrated *S*ystem, NOTIS, developed in separate modules, with acquisitions and cataloging among the first phases completed.

Public terminals allow users to find monographic titles cataloged since 1970 and practically all serials, searching by either author, title, or subject. This is the LUIS mode, *L*ibrary *U*ser *I*nformation *S*ystem, part of the NOTIS package. LUIS also gives complete information about bound volumes of periodical titles. For a current periodical all unbound issues are listed also; this feature is useful in verifying the arrival of the latest issue.

Currently there are two public terminals on the second floor and a third terminal will be installed later this year. The building's conduits enable the libary to wire for terminals on the first and third floors as well.

Circulation status information is available from the same public terminals that display catalog information. The user can learn whether an item is available before going to the bookstacks. If a book is charged out to a person or to a library function such as binding, the message on the screen tells the user when the item is due and how it may be recalled or saved.

Books can be charged out readily on a self-service machine because all faculty, students, and staff receive plastic identification badges that are machine-readable. For renewals and for persons who have been issued temporary paper badges, the user number can be typed in by a circulation assistant.

In addition to the LUIS user mode available at the public terminals, NOTIS also has a staff mode. Online check-in of periodical issues, claim requests, and payment data for periodical invoices are entered in the record by the Serials staff. All current periodicals are checked in at a terminal on the day of arrival. Each piece is "Tattle-Taped" with a thin metallic strip before being shelved. The taping process has reduced the number of "missing" issues.

## *Microforms*

The microform area was designed to be convenient, accessible, and easy to use. All equipment was donated by Bell & Howell Company. Microfilm reader/printers, microfiche reader/printers, stationary microfiche readers, and portable microfiche readers are available. The portable readers may be charged out for a limited time.

Back files for some periodicals have been purchased on 16 mm. microfilm. Each reel is enclosed in a cassette to protect the film and also to make it easier for handling. Since the number of reels is small, the extra investment in cassettes is worthwhile because a special person does not have to be hired to service the microfilm requests. Several current periodical subscriptions are received on microfiche.

## *Carrels*

Seating on all three floors is primarily in individual carrels. Much of the seating is clustered at the eastern part of the building to take advantage of the Lake Michigan view. Since there are no assigned carrels, there is a separate faculty reading room where charged out and personal material may be left.

## PROBLEMS

### Windows

The building contains large window wall areas on all sides. After construction began several small operable windows were installed on each floor because other University buildings had experienced cooling equipment failures in the past. Even if all these windows were open in the Library they would not cool the structure adequately.

### Carpeting

All floors are carpeted in the same color. The carpet squares are fire-resistant, durable, and easy to replace when needed. In order to avoid cutting the carpet pieces, some of the third floor stack ranges had to be installed several inches beyond the planned locations. The overhead fluorescent fixtures thus were centered over the tops of stack ranges, rather than being positioned over the aisles as expected.

### Lighting

If the Library had been built a year later, fluorescent lighting would not have been used so abundantly. As an energy saving measure some of the fixtures now contain fewer lights.

### Photocopy Rooms

An unforseen difficulty arose over the dissipation of the heat generated by the photocopy machines. In designing these facilities it was assumed that the ventilation would be adequate. The cooling and ventilating system will have to be modified to correct this situation.

## CONCLUSION

The building shows the result of careful preliminary planning; there have been no real deficiencies or omissions. The open uncluttered arrangement, highlighted by varied colors, has made the Library attractive to both users and staff.

# Facilities
# of the Kresge Engineering Library
# at the University of California, Berkeley

Patricia Davitt Maughan

**ABSTRACT.** A description is given of the history, planning, development and features of the Kresge Engineering Library of the University of California at Berkeley.

## *INTRODUCTION*

Groundbreaking ceremonies for the Bechtel Engineering Center, containing the Kresge Engineering Library, took place in the summer of 1978. Planning for these facilities began some five years earlier, when the former Dean of the College of Engineering at the University of California, Berkeley, appointed a committee to investigate and determine space requirements within the College.

The committee identified three major space needs, one of which was the construction of a central engineering facility which would make possible, among other things, the expansion of the library. It was anticipated that the other two projects, largely involving renovations to existing space, could be funded through state support. The third project, a new engineering center and library, was designated by the University Chancellor as a high priority on the Berkeley campus; both Fundraising and Building Committees were appointed in 1975.

The initial Building Committee's membership included representatives from the College of Engineering's administration, fac-

Patricia Davitt Maughan is Associate Librarian, Engineering Library, University of California, Berkeley. She has a BA degree from the University of Santa Clara and the MLSIS degree from Pratt Institute. Information for this article was generously provided by David M. Brown, Executive Officer, College of Engineering, and Gloria Novak, Library Space Planner.

ulty, students, the library, and the Faculty Library Committee. Ex-officio members included the Director of Facilities Management, the Campus Architect, the Berkeley Libraries' Space Planner, and alumni. The Committee was charged with developing a project planning guide, to document problems associated with the existing space configuration within the college and the library, to propose solutions, and define space requirements within the new center.

## RATIONALE

The College of Engineering is spread throughout eight main buildings in the northeast corner of campus. Many of the organized research units associated with the College are housed at the Richmond Field Station, approximately ten miles north of campus. In 1975, the College comprised some 3,200 undergraduate and graduate students, over 200 faculty, 7 academic departments, and 6 interdisciplinary programs.

During the five years preceding the Building Committee's work, some fundamental changes had taken place in engineering education at Berkeley. The College perceived a need to train its graduates to deal competently with increasingly complex technical problems, and proposed doing so by combining instruction in the traditional areas of engineering with a broader comprehension of those methods and approaches used not only in other engineering disciplines, but in fields outside of engineering as well. The College of Engineering pioneered this interdisciplinary approach to engineering education, establishing programs in environmental studies, energy, urban systems, bioengineering, and ocean engineering.

To confront the difficulties associated with the dispersion of problem solving units, defined as faculty, students, practicing engineers, and the community at large, a central facility was proposed. The Committee's plan focused on a series of agreed upon objectives: (1) to expand library facilities; (2) to provide a focal point for the Interdisciplinary Studies Program and a meeting place for students and the professional engineering community; (3) to facilitate large conferences and meetings; (4) to provide a center for student activities and organizations; and (5) to serve the community at large, by offering a center for continuing engineering education programs and by providing information services through the library.

## THE FORMER LIBRARY

It was clear that changes were required to the existent engineering library to achieve these goals. The space formerly allocated to the library totalled 6,125 square feet, very little of which was designed for use as an information providing facility. Servicing a student population of more than 3,000, the library at that time accommodated only 128 study stations, many of which were positioned at tables adjacent to an active Circulation and Reserves desk, reference collection, and the library's entrance. The remaining space was divided into 3,301 square feet of stack space, 2,175 square feet of reading room, 242 square feet of staff work area (~60 square feet per staff member), and 319 square feet allocated to Circulation and Reserves.

In 1975, between 25% and 30% of the estimated 82,500 volumes in the Engineering collection was shelved in storage at the Richmond Field Station, some ten miles away, and available only by a student staffed courier service requiring one or more days delay in servicing. In addition, the circulation policy in effect during those years was biased toward keeping materials out of the library, for want of shelf space. The Building Committee perceived this as a situation requiring change.

## THE INITIAL PROPOSAL

College officials felt their needs required a library at least 2½ times larger, providing additional seating for 340, and new equipment with which to access information. The original building proposal called for a library of 15,000 square feet, with stack space for 90,000 volumes to permit the return of materials from storage and to allow for revisions to the library's loan policies. The goal was to provide for greater availability of materials on site. In addition, the proposal called for increasing the staff work area to 500 square feet, the librarian's office to 200 square feet, and the reading area to 6,200 square feet. Rather than a single reading room, separate areas were envisioned for reference, current periodicals, leisure reading, open reserves, microform equipment, computer terminals, and public use typewriters: 8,000 square feet were earmarked for the general stacks. Later in the planning and design process, nearly all of these figures were adjusted upwards.

The library was only one part of the program planning guide. The other parts called for central offices and lounge areas for the engineering student organizations, 5,000 square feet of space for Interdisciplinary Studies, and a 300 seat auditorium, with a broad range of video equipment for conferences and seminars.

## FUNDRAISING

With a skeletal proposal in mind, the College launched an unprecedented private fundraising campaign for the project, with anticipated construction costs of $5 million. A significant portion of the fundraising drive was directed at some 18,000 U.C. Berkeley Engineering alumni. Both the Bechtel and Kresge foundations were solicited for grants to be matched by alumni donations. The concept of challenge grants to the alumni brought very favorable results.

## COMMUNITY RESISTANCE
## AND THE ENVIRONMENTAL IMPACT STUDY

With success on the fundraising front, plans continued to evolve for the facility. By early 1977, the design had developed to the point where a site had been chosen, and schematics, development and preliminary drawings had been completed.

During roughly this same period, the Berkeley Architectural Heritage Association and members of the Berkeley campus and community filed a complaint with the County Superior Court, objecting to the proposed site which would necessitate the demolition of the Naval Architecture Building, designed by John Galen Howard, before construction on the new Engineering Center could begin. Following these and other objections, a series of public hearings was scheduled and held, and an Environmental Impact

Study was commissioned and completed. As part of the study, four to five alternative sites for the Engineering Center were examined. With time, the Naval Architecture Building was added to the National Register of Historic Places, and an alternate site was selected by the University Chancellor.

Once the new site was agreed upon, a smaller Building Committee including the Assistant Deans, the Budget and Planning Officer, a student representative, the Chair of the Faculty Library Committee, Director of Facilities Management, and Library Space Planner was reconstituted by the Dean, to finalize plans for the center. Preliminary and working drawings were developed and a structural engineer was engaged to work on structural plans, heating, ventilation, and other required utilities. Plans were approved by the Regents in 1978 and the dedication of the Bechtel Engineering Center and Kresge Engineering Library took place in June of 1980.

## THE NEW LIBRARY

The Kresge Engineering Library shares ground level space in the Bechtel Center with some of the College's conference rooms and a student lounge. The floor above houses a 300 seat auditorium, additional lounge space, and offices for Interdisciplinary Studies, College Publications, and engineering student organizations. The top floor of the Center is the site of an outdoor cafe/restaurant for campus use.

Because of refinements made in the final building plan, much of the library's 21,841 square feet was built underground. With so many of the campus utility lines located on or near the site, possibilities for space utilization were constrained. As a result, the architect chose to use vertical rather than horizontal space for expansion, and 12,352 square feet of multitiered shelving were constructed and installed in such a way that the library's upstairs mezzanine is supported by lower level stacks.

The new library is an attractive and popular center for study and research on the Berkeley campus. Fully carpeted and constructed on four levels, it is totally accessible to the handicapped through a series of ramps designed by the architect. Two hundred sixty-five user stations are provided throughout the library, and separate service points are staffed at the library's entrance for both Circulation and Reference functions. (See Figures 1 & 2.)

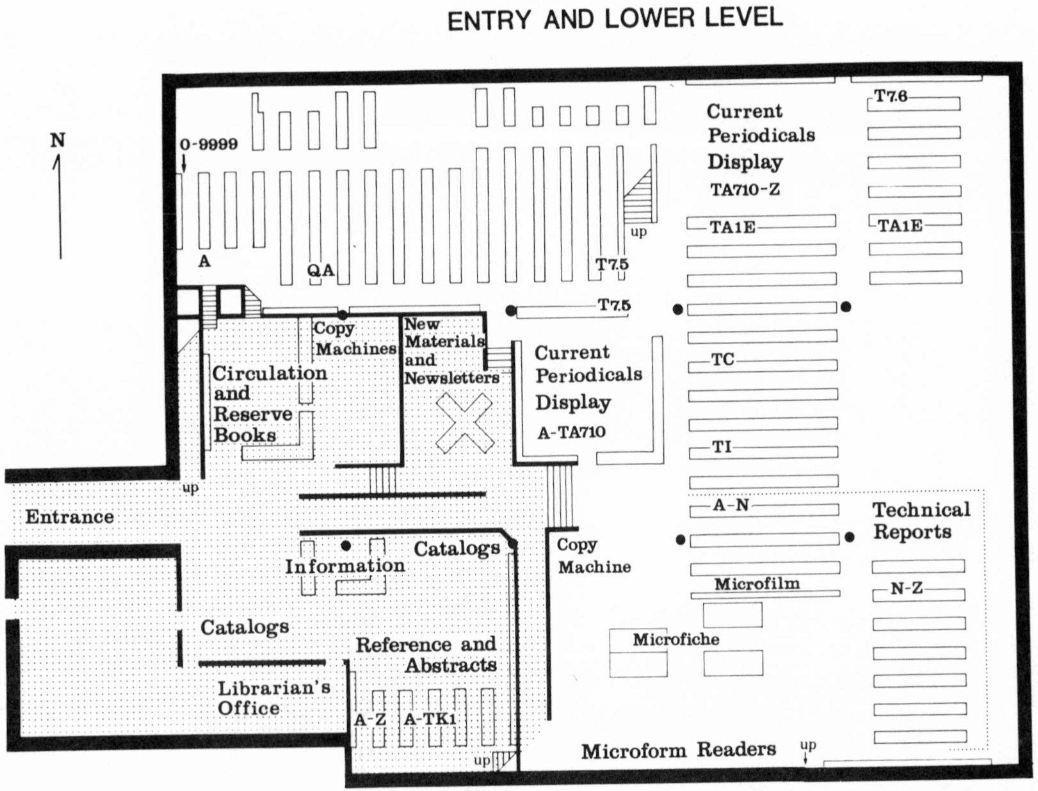
ENTRY AND LOWER LEVEL
N
0-9999
A
QA
T7.5
up
T7.5
Current
Periodicals
Display
TA710-Z
T7.6
TA1E
TA1E
TC
TI
A-N
Technical
Reports
N-Z
Microfilm
Microfiche
Microform Readers
up
Copy
Machines
New
Materials
and
Newsletters
Circulation
and
Reserve
Books
Current
Periodicals
Display
A-TA710
up
Entrance
Information
Catalogs
Copy
Machine
Catalogs
Reference and
Abstracts
Librarian's
Office
A-Z
A-TK1
up
UPPER LEVEL ON REVERSE SIDE

FIGURE 1.

FIGURE 2.
(Photo by Anne Terrell)

In addition to study carrels, the 6,752 square feet of user space accommodates current periodical display and reading areas for some 3,360 currently received titles. The shelving areas provide space for approximately 90,000 volumes of stack materials, including an estimated 1,350 volume Reference and Reserve collections. Approximately 24,000 of lesser used volumes remain in storage, and are accessible via campus courier service.

When planning for the new library, a decision was made to transfer a majority of the Libraries' technical reports in microform and paper copy from the Government Documents Department to the Engineering Library. The College of Engineering supported library plans calling for the utilization of new technologies wherever possible, and funded the purchase of two Minolta RP 405 and one Minolta RP 407 microform reader/printers, a Bruning OP 10 microfiche duplicator, and a 3M 261/262 Duplifiche printer and developer. In addition, some 15 microfiche reader stations, located throughout the library, are used to access both the technical report collection and the University of California, Berkeley, Libraries' Catalog 2, a union catalog available on microfiche.

Additional hardware purchased for and available in the library include a portable Texas Instruments Silent 700 miniterm for on-line searching of RLIN and commercially available databases, and a hardwired CRT MELVYL terminal. MELVYL is a prototype on-line catalog, developed by the University of California's Division of Library Automation, containing selected records from the nine University of California Campus Libraries.

As of June 1982, the Engineering Library's collection contained a total of 113,900 monographs, 3,360 currently received serials, and 491,000 technical reports in microform and paper copy.

The library's staff is currently composed of 2 FTE librarians, 4 full time library assistants, and approximately 4 FTE student assistants.

Continuing its generous base of support evidenced in funding the construction of the Kresge Engineering Library, the College of Engineering has provided funds on a two-year, experimental basis, to support free microform copying facilities to the Berkeley campus, a half-time Engineering Database Services Librarian, and extended library hours.

Two years following the dedication of the Bechtel Engineering Center, nearly all of the plans and ideas envisioned some ten years ago have been realized. An expanded library, with an annual circulation of nearly 77,000, utilizes current technologies to provide information services to the Berkeley College of Engineering, the San Francisco Bay Area's professional engineering community, and the public at large. The Center supports annual university-industry conferences, an active continuing engineering education program, and numerous interdisciplinary seminars.

# Facilities of Swarthmore College's Science and Engineering Library

Michael J. Durkan
Emi K. Horikawa

**ABSTRACT.** Building a science library for Swarthmore College is described in its various stages: from estimating space needs to moving into the completed building.

## *BACKGROUND*

Swarthmore College was founded in 1864 by members of the Society of Friends as a co-educational institution. It is situated in the borough of Swarthmore on some 300 acres of rolling, wooded land about fifteen miles to the southeast of Philadelphia. The College's location makes possible cooperation with three nearby institutions, Bryn Mawr and Haverford Colleges and the University of Pennsylvania. Enrollment is limited to about 1,300 men and women students. The Course and External Examination (Honors) Programs both seek to evoke the maximum effort and development from each student. The Honors Program, in which Swarthmore pioneered, has as its main ingredients close association with faculty members, often in small seminars, concentrated work in various fields of study, and maximum latitude for the development of individual responsibility.

The College Libraries consist of the following units: McCabe Library (the general collection), the Cornell Library of Science and Engineering, the Observatory Library, the Underhill Music Library, the Friends Historical Library (a collection of Quaker materials)

Michael J. Durkan is College Librarian, Swarthmore College, Swarthmore, PA 19081. He has an undergraduate degree in Latin and Irish from St. Patrick's College, Maynooth, and a Diploma in Library Science from University College, Dublin. Emi K. Horikawa is Science Librarian at Swarthmore College. She has a BS in Chemistry and Biology from the University of Nevada, and an MA in Biochemistry from the University of Utah.

and the Peace Collection. The latter two are housed within the McCabe Library. Together they amount to some 600,000 volumes and some 2,800 periodical subscriptions. The newest unit is the Cornell Library of Science and Engineering, dedicated in December 1982 and housing some 60,000 volumes of 530 periodical subscriptions.

The early history of library accommodation for Science and Engineering at Swarthmore College is similar to that of most institutions. Small departmental collections were established in each departmental office. Borrowing and use was pretty much left to the individual faculty member, student use was not greatly marked. These satellite libraries were maintained by a librarian from the main college library on a weekly basis. In 1959 a new building was provided to house the departments of Chemistry, Mathematics and Physics. It was felt that this would be a good time to gather together the library materials for these departments as well as for Engineering and house them in an area developed especially for their use. The Library was not represented on the planning committee and had minimal input on space and arrangement. The space devoted to the Library was a rectangular room of some 5,000 square feet which included a small office for the Librarian. The Librarian with supporting staff of 1.5 people and student assistants was responsible for the administration of the DuPont Science Library as well as for the departmental collections housed in the departments of Astronomy and Biology which were still operating as departmental libraries. The Observatory Library has a handsome reading room with wooden shelves which resembles a private library. Bound periodicals are shelved in this room with current periodicals placed on the table for browsing. In a separate room there are shelves for additional bound periodicals, monographs and publications from observatories around the world. This library is small and intimate and will remain as a separate departmental library administered from the science library.

By the end of ten years, space in the DuPont Library was filled to capacity. The main problem was how to exist and provide service in the face of a growing collection with no provision for expansion. Storage was the immediate answer. Certain periodical titles were designated whose back files were sent to be housed in the Central Library; some monographs were stored in an area allocated to the Science Library by the department of Chemistry. Weeding was a continuing activity. These were however only stop-gap measures. It was clear that additional space was needed for books, for readers and for staff.

In Spring 1977, a formal request was sent from the Library via the Library Committee to the College Administration, recommending that "the Science Collections now in Martin (biology) and DuPont be integrated in adequate quarters. . ." The response was positive, indicating the possibility that renovation of existing space might be a solution. This option was explored at length, as were those of incorporating the Science Library and services in an addition to the Main Library or of expanding the DuPont Library. By January 1980, all these had been discarded in favor of a separate, new facility. A committee with representation from the Library, the College administration and the science faculty, was established to choose the architect for the project. By January 1981, the Philadelphia firm H2L2 Architects/Planners had been designated as the architects of the proposed new building. The Paul Restall Company of Swarthmore was chosen as the construction company for the facility which would be ready for use by September 1982.

The program presented to the architects called for a building that would house library materials and make them readily available to users. Other expectations were as follows: the new library would be flexible, friendly, warm and pleasant; it would be a live, vital place, capable of growth and change; special emphasis would be placed on the library as an active participant in the teaching and learning program; since most of the materials would be open to readers, the design would provide the greatest possible access to them; there would be high use of the building for study since most of the students, the prime users, would be living on campus. Special attention would be paid to periodicals—both for storage and display; to microforms; and to the increasing use of technology encompassing on-line retrieval, together with other innovations. Both individual and group seating and lounge areas would be provided; lighting, environmental controls and floor coverings also were specified. The space requirements for each area and activity were specified in detail, accompanied by a text indicating its special needs and its particular function. The architects were also provided with check lists of items of special concern which would not be covered in the program statements: telephones, signs, clocks, bookdrop, keys, electrical outlets, etc. The final document provided was a "Space Requirements Summary" listing the square footage for each area with an overall total of 13,210 square feet.

## PLANNING

Once the architectural firm had been chosen, a series of weekly meetings were initiated—attended by the architects, the College Engineer, the College Librarian and the Science Librarian. The site decided on lay between the Library's greatest users: biology, on the one side; physics, chemistry and mathematics on the other. It also overlooked the Crum Woods, an area of great unspoiled, natural beauty. A three-story building was chosen so as to minimize the building footprint on this particular site. The details were worked out swiftly and efficiently, the Library presenting its needs and requirements, the architects incorporating them in their planning, and the College Engineer determining their feasibility and conformity with local ordinances.

During this process, advice was continually sought from all constituencies through correspondence and meetings with various groups of faculty, students, administration and library staff. The building folder from the American Library Association was obtained on interlibrary loan; much advice, solicited and otherwise, was received. The staff of the College Library provided much valuable information. Their specific suggestions included: carpeted floors for comfort and quiet; operable windows; drains for floors of rest rooms; overhead carrel lighting separate from individual carrel lights; a vestibule to serve as a weather-lock and with a recessed mat to remove outside snow and grime before entering; lockable book drop and special shelving. Based as they were on practical experience, their opinions were especially useful and were invariably followed in detail.

Recognizing that the prime users would be students and faculty, we at every stage, both formally and informally, solicited their opinions. Both constituencies were represented on the initial planning committee and were brought in again at the various stages of development, e.g., interior decoration and furniture selection. Student concerns were also voiced frequently in informal conversations at the circulation desk and at the study tables in the DuPont Library. Some were especially useful, others not so—we listened to them all and showed the students we welcomed their suggestions. Their comments had a wide range including: wide arms on lounge chairs to facilitate reading and notetaking; single carrels as against double or modular carrels; group study tables; a coffee corner; climate control and color of carpeting. Individual faculty members tended to communicate more by memo— there was very little written response from students. Faculty wrote concerning the placement of the building, access to the library's loading dock, walkways linking the library with other buildings, consultation space for periodicals both current and bound, climate control, seminar rooms to meet with students.

## CONSTRUCTION PHASE

During construction as soon as the exterior has been completed and when the interior arrangement is in recognizable shape it is important that the Librarian should visit the site frequently. Since the Librarian knows the specific requirements, she/he can keep an eye out to make sure that the specifications are observed in all deail and to see that they are corrected if they vary. We found that this was best achieved by contacting the College Engineer and having him make representations to the architects or to the construction firm. In some cases the architect was approached directly by the Librarian. There were many details which were rectified at that stage which would have been next to impossible to take care of in the completed building. Some deviations from our specifications which we were able to rectify in this manner were: operable windows; removal of shelving which would interfere with the placement of microform readers and printers, unsuitable doors on offices and seminar rooms. The construction phase was extremely important, and the Librarian helped the final product immeasurably by frequent visits to the site during that time. The building progressed according to schedule. Occupancy was expected by September 1982; on August 4th and 5th the contents (books, files, etc.) were moved into the completed building, well ahead of the schedule.

## COMPLETED BUILDING

The structure is flat slab floors supported by round concrete columns and 8″ CMU bearing walls. Interior partitions are of exposed concrete block and drywall. there are aluminum curtain walls at front and back. The floor coverings are of carpet and ceramic title. A rich magenta color was chosen for the carpet to contrast with the grey concrete interiors, while lounge furniture is in shades of purple, green and red. The wooden furniture (current periodical shelving, card catalog, carrels, chairs) is of light oak. Some of the furniture from the DuPont Library was refinished for use in the new building, as was the metal shelving for the bound periodicals on the upper level. Ceilings are exposed on the lower and main levels, leaving the air ducts and other conduits in full view. The air ducts are painted in a shade of very light purple to harmonize with the magenta carpet. The library has net area of 16,770 sq. ft., with a seating capacity of 178 and a volume capacity of 120,000 volumes.

The three-level design of the building places current periodicals, reference, card catalog and administration on the entry level, sandwiched between bound periodicals and microforms on the upper level and monographs on the lower level. As can be seen from Figure 1, on the first floor the current periodicals surround an area of comfortable lounge seating overlooking the lower level and with an unobstructed view to the woods outside. Nearby is the reference desk with an online search terminal, the card catalog leading to the reference area with indexes and abstracts, with study and consultation tables along the front wall. To the left as you enter is the staff and administrative area with the Circulation Desk (concrete block with oak top) extending outwards. Behind the circulation desk along the wall are the staff lounge, staff office, Librarian's office and seminar room. The staff area has a view of the circulation desk which can be closed off as desired. Doors open to the public area, giving a sense of closeness and approachability to library users. The seminar room with blackboards and projection screen, is fitted for computer terminals. It was designed for small gatherings of about ten people and is already in much demand. The ceramic tile floor surrounds this whole area and acts as a pathway to the top of the stairs leading to the lower level. A coffee corner for student and faculty use is located immediately to the left as you enter the Library. In it are located a counter, sink, hot plate and cabinets. Seating from the old Biology Library has been placed in this tiled area—hot beverages are forbidden outside of this location. This student-run service is much appreciated and is regarded as a special privilege. Close to the coffee corner is the photocopy

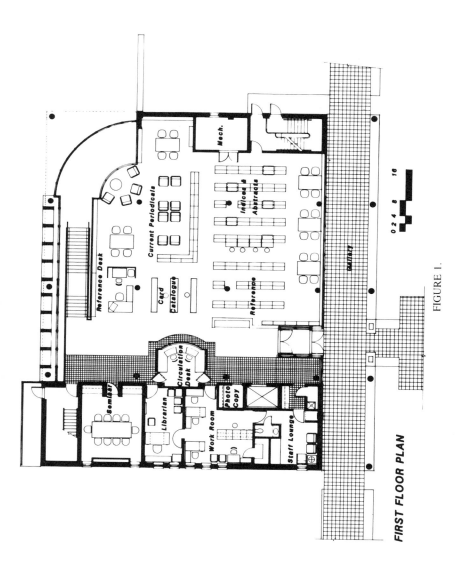

FIRST FLOOR PLAN

FIGURE 1.

101

machine placed within an area designed to minimize noise, with counter space and storage for supplies.

A broad carpeted staircase leads to the lower level which houses the monograph collection arranged in L.C. class order. (See Figure 2) The stair leads to a lounge area with a large semicircular window looking out on the woods. Study space in this level is devoted mostly to large study tables with some individual carrels tucked under the stairway. The Sigma Xi Room, a seminar room fitted by the local chapter, is located on this floor together with two typing rooms and two rooms to serve the handicapped. Entrance to the top level is by either of two stairwells on the entrance level. This is the largest of the three floors with individual carrels along two sides. Bound periodicals, arranged alphabetically by title, are shelved here. The microforms room is located at one end adjacent to three lockable study carrels. Group study seating, a lounge area (with a student-run, uncataloged science fiction collection) and public restrooms complete the arrangements on this level. The clerestory at the front of the building brings much natural light onto this floor, giving it an airy feeling, emphasized by the aluminum ribbed ceiling which extends throughout the entire clerestory both inside and out. This is the place for quiet, concentrated study and research in contrast to the varying busyness of the other two floors.

## GENERAL COMMENTS

As a working library the building is functional and pleasant. The general layout seems to work well—the arrangement of functions and of the collection is clear, direct and easily understood. The small library atmosphere combined with the spacious accommodations provides a pleasing environment for study, research and browsing. The use of some furnishings from the old library gives a sense of continuity and the presence of old friends. The division by floors has underlined the differences in the study habits of the students. Those who cannot work except in busy surroundings will usually be found on the entrance or lower levels, others who require absolute calm and quiet will opt for the carrels and tables on the top level.

Since the Library seeks to be an active partner in teaching and

FIGURE 2.

learning, the building in its openness and in its accommodation to students provides the climate for learning. The staff, the book collection, online search facilities, microforms, and catalogs are all easily accessible. The spirit of inquiry is facilitated by the availability of the services and materials housed in the building. On all floors in the study carrels (both locked and open), in the seminar rooms and in the microforms room provision has been made for the addition of computer terminals. We expect to be installing the terminals on a gradual basis within the next year.

Zoned climate controls are used, allowing for the minimum of energy to be used especially during vacation periods. There is a solar domestic hot water system. Much natural light comes into the building on all levels. Where this is not sufficient, individual range and carrel lights also control energy use.

The building is set into a bank overlooking the Crum Woods, an area of fine natural, unspoiled beauty. Staff, students and faculty are very happy with the facility and show their pleasure by their frequent use of it. It has lured some humanists and social scientists inside its doors to conduct seminars there. The building is named for its donors, Julien Cornell & Virginia Stratton Cornell, both members of the class of 1930.

## REFERENCES

The following publications were consulted in the preparation of the program and statement for the architect:

Cohen, Aaron; Cohen, E. *Designing and space planning for libraries: a behavioral guide.* New York: Bowker; 1979.

Dayton, Irving E. The Pierre S. duPont Science building, Swarthmore College. *American Journal of Physics.* 29 (11): 753-763; 1961 Nov.

Mason, Ellsworth. *Mason on library buidings.* Metuchen, N.J.: Scarecrow Press; 1980.

Metcalf, Keyes D. *Planning academic and research library buildings.* New York: McGraw-Hill; 1965.

Thompson, Godfrey. *Planning and design of library buildings.* 2d ed. London: Architectural Press; 1977.

# NEW REFERENCE WORKS IN SCIENCE AND TECHNOLOGY

Janice W. Bain, Editor

*Reviewers for this issue are: Barbara Walcott, Health Sciences Library, (BW) and Ellis Mount, School of Library Service, (EM), both of Columbia University, New York, NY.*

## BIOLOGY

Davis, Elizabeth B. *Using the biological literature.* New York: Dekker; 1981. 286p. $33.50. ISSB 0-8247-1354-5.

This guide was developed from a series of handouts designed to introduce biology students at the University of Illinois Urbana-Champaign to the biological sciences literature. A comprehensive list of important sources, it assumes some understanding of the structure of the scientific literature. The arrangement is by areas of specialization, such as genetics, and then by form of material, e.g., handbook, dictionary, periodical. Most chapters begin with a list of the major subject headings used by the Library of Congress, Medical Subject Headings, and/or BioSciences Information Service that are appropriate to the subject. Entries are annotated, but only where they first appear. Subsequent listings of the same source refer back to the annotated one. The annotations are informative and some are critical. If a source is available online, that is noted. There are two introductory chapters, one on the history of the biological literature, the other on

Janice W. Bain is Program Review Coordinator at the Transportation Research Board, National Research Council of the National Academy of Sciences, 2101 Constitution Avenue, Washington, DC 20418.

subject headings. The index provides access by author, title, or general topic. It is unfortunate that the poor typography selected by the publisher detracts from the content. (BW)


## DENTISTRY

Jablonski, Stanley. *Illustrated dictionary of dentistry*. Philadelphia: Saunders; 1982. 919p. $39.50. ISBN 0-7216-5055-4.

The scope of this new dictionary is wider than is indicated by the title, for it defines terms from fields of science and technology related to dentistry in addition to the terminology of dental and health care. In format it follows the leading medical dictionaries. Most entries consist of a phonetic spelling, etymological source, a definition and synonyms if there are any. Multi-word terms are clustered under the noun that is part of the term. Trade names, acronyms, and personal names are included. Definitions are as short as one line or as long as half a page. The illustrations are drawings, tables, and some photographs, and they are not abundant. There are several appendices: lists of accredited educational programs in dentistry and allied fields, descriptions of the American and Canadian Dental Associations, and tables of laboratory reference values. All the material presented in the Dictionary has been reviewed by the consultants whose names appear in the front of the book. Though its primary use will be in dentistry, this source should also prove valuable as a supplement to medical and other science dictionaries. (BW)


## INFORMATION SYSTEMS

*Encyclopedia of information systems and services*. 5th ed. Edited by John Schmittroth, Jr. Detroit: Gale; 1982. 2 vols. $260.00. ISBN 0-8103-1138-0.

A basic reference tool which provides more than 2500 entries describing abstracting/indexing services, online search services, reference service agencies and the like. Many sci-tech subjects, ranging from aeronautics to zoology and located on a global basis (Australia to Yugoslovia), are included. Each entry gives the name of the organization, a description of the service, its scope, important collection highlights, publications issued, computer-based products and names of those to contact. (EM)


# TOXICOLOGY

Wexler, Philip. *Information resources in toxicology.* New York: Elsevier; 1982. 333p. $45.00. ISBN 0-444-00616-8.

Although toxicology has a large and rapidly growing literature, this is the first guide to its information sources. It should be very useful. Wexler defines toxicology broadly, and includes sources on radiation hazards, occupational medicine, analytical techniques, and other related areas as well as the more obvious subjects such a poisoning and carcinogenesis. The emphasis is on chemical hazards, because of their importance, and on health effects. Materials are grouped under general headings: reference sources (print and non-print), organizations, legislation and regulations, international activities, education, information handling, and journal articles. Within each section the arrangement is by subject. Most entries are annotated. They are numbered consecutively throughout the book, and there are two subject indexes, one to the journal articles, and one to the remainder of the work. Unlike many guides to the literature, this one will provide answers to some reference questions instead of just leading to a source. For example, the section on education lists universities offering graduate programs in toxicology, and the section on legislation identifies key laws relating to the field. An appendix lists poison control centers by state. (BW)

# SCI-TECH ONLINE

Ellen Nagle, Editor

## DATABASE NEWS

### A New Version of CHEMLINE

Beginning in January 1983 a modified *CHEMLINE* file was made available to the NLM user community at a substantially reduced cost. In order to retain a valuable chemical dictionary service at a more affordable price level, NLM negotiated with Chemical Abstracts Service (CAS) to modify the *CHEMLINE* content in a manner that would allow reduced royalties. These negotiations were predicated on the belief that considerable cost savings to the users of the database and to the National Library of Medicine could be achieved without significant degradation of the utility of the service, according to NLM's Specialized Information Service.

The content of *CHEMLINE* is no longer being derived from the CAS Registry Nomenclature and Structure Service (RNSS). Instead, CAS Registry Numbers, molecular formulas, and systematic chemical names are taken from the CAS bibliographic files (*CBAC* and *CA SEARCH*) that NLM is licensed to use for its *TOXLINE* files. In addition, synonyms are now being derived from the *CA Index Guide*.

This approach to the restructuring of *CHEMLINE* means that the *CHEMLINE* royalties paid to CAS will be based on *CBAC*, *CA SEARCH* and the *CA Index Guide* rates rather than the RNSS rates. This has resulted in a royalty charge reduction from $78.97 to $32.48 per online connect hour for *CHEMLINE* usage. The new online connect charges are $54/hour for prime time and $47/hour non-prime, including NLM's charges of $22/hour and $15/hour respectively.

The restructuring of *CHEMLINE* also means a change in the number of synonyms listed for each substance in the file. The RNSS contains all non-systematic names indexed by CAS since 1965. However, the *CA Index Guide* contains non-systematic names in common usage. Therefore, the new *CHEMLINE* file will carry fewer synonyms: those which reflect common usage. All data elements, fragmentation rules, and print formats formerly used in *CHEMLINE* have been retained in the new version, allowing continuity in searching capabilities.

## SDC Offers New Metals Database

*MDF/I, METALS DATAFILE/I* is a new ORBIT database supplied by the American Society for Metals. A companion file to *METADEX, MDF/I* contains mechanical and physical properties, specification and designation numbers, compositions, and applications for ferrous and non-ferrous metals and alloys. *MDF/I* differs from conventional bibliographic files; numeric data is provided in response to the selection of an individual alloy name. *MDF/I* also allows the searcher to specify alloy classes and locate alloys with similar compositions, and to determine property variation by condition, environment, or temperature variation. Using SDC's "print hit" feature, one can print only the property subfield(s) which apply to the specific search request. Connect hour rates for *MDF/I* are $50/hour; print rates are $.10/online print; $.25/offline print, $.75/print SPEC online, $1/print SPEC offline; and $1/print full online (includes properties), $1.25/print full offline.

## BRS Develops DISC

BRS has introduced a new online table of contents service called *DISC (Data Processing and Information Science Contents)*, which provides current access to microcomputing literature in leading journals as well as access to peripherally related data on mini systems, information science and EDP. This BRS-produced database permits: quick access to the entire tables of contents of popular and professional EDP-related journals; the capability to display and print tables of contents in their entirety without referring to the printed journal; retrieval of features and regular columns in specified journals; and location of product reviews and pricing information for mainframes, micros, minis, software packages. Updated monthly, *DISC* features more than 70 searchable 2-character classification codes which facilitate subject retrieval. These codes are designed to reflect diverse subject matter (e.g., hardware, software, marketing, robotics) as well as to designate the scope of the item referenced. In addition, *DISC* includes 17 searchable publication type codes which distinguish between interviews, product reviews, advertisement, editorials, etc. The file currently contains approximately 3500 citations dating from January 1982 to the present. *DISC* is available at a $9 per connect hour royalty; citations have a royalty fee of $.07 each, printed online or offline.

### DIALOG Announces Arthur D. Little/Online

The data base of the world's oldest and largest consulting firm, Arthur D. Little, is now online as DIALOG File 192. The database is an index to the non-exclusive sources within the firm, including its divisions and subsidiaries. It provides references to industry forecasts, strategic planning, economic forecasts, company assessments, environmental developments, energy management, and emerging technologies. Reports cover a broad range of topics including chemicals and related products (food, agribusiness, forest products, packaging, plastic and fibers, environment), construction and building, consumer products and services, electronics, health care (pharmaceuticals, medical supplies and equipment, diagnostic products), information processing, telecommunications, and transportation. In addition to basic bibliographic information on the reports, each record includes a table of contents, a list of tables in the publications, and a list of the figures, if any.

The database is prepared by Arthur D. Little Decision Resources, a subsidiary of the parent company, and includes material from several of their industry reports and newsletters. *Arthur D. Little/Online* contains approximately 250 records and will be updated monthly. The price is $90 per connect hour, $.20 per bibliographic record printed offline, and $100 for a detailed summary printed either online or offline.

### NHPIC Data Added to the HEALTH File

The National Health Planning Information Center (NHPIC) in cooperation with the National Library of Medicine has added 9,451 document citations to the *HEALTH* file effective May 1983. The documents cited are all English-language, non-journal publications in the health planning area and have been previously cited in *Weekly Government Abstracts: Health Planning Series*, which is published by NTIS. Most of the documents are technical reports; the remainder are monographs, monographic chapters, or theses. The years of publication covered in this retrospective addition are 1975–1981; *MeSH* headings used correspond to the 1983 *MeSH*. Special search features of the NHPIC record include document ordering numbers and procurement sources, publication types, and corporate names.

## PUBLICATIONS AND SEARCH AIDS

### New Chemical Tool for MEDLINE

The National Library of Medicine has announced the availability of *Medical Subject Headings—Supplementary Chemical Records*, a new search tool for *MEDLINE*. The 975-page publication which supplements the D category of *Medical Subject Headings (MeSH)*, contains records of approximately 25,000 chemicals which have been identified in journals indexed for *MEDLINE* between 1970 and November 1982. However, records of chemicals cited only once before 1978 and not again since then are not included, in order to limit the publication to a manageable size.

The *"Chemical Tool"* as it is known does not contain any of the chemical descriptors that are in the D category of *MeSH*, nor any terms which are synonyms for *MeSH* descriptors. The latter are found in the printed *MeSH* as "see" references. Information provided for each chemical compound listed includes the generic name, where possible; synonyms which have been identified in articles indexed for *MEDLINE*; CAS Registry Number or Enzyme Commission Number; the *MeSH* heading under which citations on the chemical are indexed; and additional information concerning pharmacological activities attributed to the chemical, indexing notes, and other data considered potentially useful in identifying and characterizing a particular chemical substance. The publication may be ordered from the National Technical Information Service, Springfield, VA 22161. The price is $22 for hard copy and $4.50 for microfiche; the order number is PB83-140640.

## EDUCATION

### BIOSIS Introduces New Medical Specialty Training

The BioSciences Information Service (BIOSIS) is offering a new training course entitled Med/BIOSIS. Designed for librarians, information scientists and medical research specialists, this course will teach techniques for retrieving information on specific medical topics from the more than five million bibliographic references in the *BIOSIS Previews* database. *BIOSIS Previews* is considered a major source of information on medical research. Med/BIOSIS is the third in a series of subject specialty courses designed to assist users in searching individual subject fields within BIOSIS' multi-subject biological and biomedical database. Course instruction topics include details on the BIOSIS medical coverage, index organization, strategy design and effective retrieval of specific medical topics. Other BIOSIS specialty courses are available for the pharmaceutical and agricultural fields. All BIOSIS training courses are offered free of charge. For more information about Med/BIOSIS and other BIOSIS training courses, contact the BIOSIS Education and Training Group, 2100 Arch St., Philadelphia PA, 19103-1399.

## FOURTH NATIONAL ONLINE MEETING

The fourth National Online Meeting was held in New York City, April 12-14, 1983. The 3-day program featured more than 150 technical papers and product review presentations. Downloading, online pricing, electronic publishing, and microcomputers were among the topics covered. Details of the meeting will be forthcoming in our next column.

# SCI-TECH IN REVIEW

Suzanne Fedunok, Editor

## TIME ANALYSIS STUDY

Beecher, J.W.; Self, P.C.; Stinson, E.R.; Anderson, N.D. Use of random alarm mechanisms for analyzing professional and support activities in science libraries: methodology. *Library Research.* 4(2): 137–146; Summer 1982.

Ranstine, F.A., Davis, E.B., Hulsizer, B., and Williams, M. Use of random alarm mechanisms for analyzing professional and support activities in science libraries: data and discussion. *Library Research.* 4(2): 147–161, Summer 1982.

The authors report on a two semester long time analysis study of the activities of the public services staff in the science libraries of the University of Illinois at Urbana Champaign. The study was designed to show the "possible relationships between staff activities and computer literature searching (a new service), the budget allocated to the science libraries, the Library Computer System of online circulation records (implemented during the study), the relationship between staff size and professional librarian's research and publication activities, and the level of public service and technical service activities in the decentralized departmental libraries.

The assumption of the science and technology librarians was that there would be a discontinuation of traditional patterns of work because of the changes in the library staff and the need for them to learn new assignments, the changed focus of the library administration, and the necessity for the professional staff to be involved in "activities not directly related to job performance."

Data were collected using Random Alarm Mechanisms (RAMs),

which are battery powered devices that beep at random intervals. The library staff were instructed to mark down what they were doing at the time of the alarm on a summary sheet of 65 categories of library activities. Although there was not enough information collected to make firm conclusions about some of the things the group wanted to study, there were some unexpected findings: there seemed to be no relationship between the size of the staff and the percentage of time spent on public services or technical services activities; there seemed to be no relationship between the size of library budget and the amount of time spent on acquisitions activities; also, there seemed to be a surprising amount of time—up to 30 per cent in some units—spent on technical services activities, despite the designation of the science and technology libraries as a "public service unit." Finally, the study showed that the librarians spent a "generally low percentage of their time" (about ten percent) on reference activities.

## *INTERDISCIPLINARY SCIENCE*

Pachevsky, T. Problems of information services with respect to integration of the sciences. *Journal of the American Society for Information Science* 33(3): 115–123; 1982 May.

The author reports on a survey in which 432 specialists in science from 16 countries responded to a "closed-type" questionnaire on how they met their information needs, and how they rated the information services to scientists in their countries. One third of the researchers reported that their research was of a complex interdisciplinary nature, and this group proved to be the most dissatisfied with the existing level of information service in their fields.

Responses to the questionnaire were correlated to the level of economic development of the country in which the researcher works, to reveal a high percentage of dissatisfied interdisciplinary scientists in all countries, and a higher level of dissatisfaction among scientists working in developing countries.

The author's study showed also that while in the United States domestic abstract journals are the main source of information to researchers, in Europe the use of domestic and foreign abstract journals is about equal, while in small developing countries there is a heavy dependence on foreign abstracting journals as sources of scientific information. The conclusion reached is that "the main problem of information services in our time is the problem of satisfying the information needs of specialists working in the field of interdisciplinary scientific trends."

## HISTORY OF ABSTRACTING AND INDEXING SERVICES

Cooper, M. Secondary information services in science and technology: a wide-angle view. *Journal of the American Society for Information Science*. 33(3): 152–156; 1982 May.

This article, from the "Perspectives on . . ." section of the journal, gives a brief history of the scientific and technical abstracting and indexing journals since world War II. It underlines the emergence, especially after Sputnik in 1957, of "mission-oriented and interdisciplinary science," and of government produced or sponsored secondary information publications to deal with this trend. The article concludes with comments on the relationship between secondary services and libraries, which soon became their primary customers. "Information centers and libraries, both academic and special have already cancelled subscriptions to some printed services, primarily because of their high cost. They are expecting to fulfill their secondary information needs through database searching. The number of available terminals, however, in most of these institutions is still limited, thus requiring an intermediary (information professional) to perform searches at his/her convenience. Until most searchers can have access to a terminal and can conduct their own searches, if they so desire, creative browsing and individual access will be limited. Although the paperless electronic library is clearly on the horizon, the road might be long and rocky before we arrive there."

## PUBLICATION COUNTS AND RESEARCH TRENDS

David, H.G.; Piip, L.; Haly, A.R. Examination of research trends by analysis of publication numbers. *Journal of Information Science*. 3(6): 283–288; 1981 December.

The authors used publication counts derived from manual and online searches of the literature to obtain data on trends in textile research, and in particular to document a trend away from pure research toward applied research. Data were collected on the number and categories of publications in periodicals and on the number of patents filed from 1969–1979. The authors correlated the number of patents for any year to the number of papers abstracted or published that year, and found a significant positive correlation among subjects of research.

Using *CA Condensates* as part of their project, the authors also discovered what the publishers called an interesting "artefact" of the database: for two years of their study the total numbers of abstracts found in the database were half the number found in the printed abstracts. While the authors warn of the short comings of counts of scientific papers to do bibliometric research, they emphasize the advantages of its directness and simplicity and feel the kind of study they conducted might be undertaken for other subjects as well.

## COST-BENEFIT ANALYSIS OF LIBRARY SERVICES

Kantor, P.B. Levels of output related to cost of operation of scientific and technical libraries. *Library Research*. 3(1): 1–28; 1981 Spring; 3(2): 141–154; 1981 Summer.

The author summarized the final report of the LORCOST libraries project issued from Case-Western Reserve University. The study concluded that the levels of service and operating costs of scientific and technical libraries can be described by an econometric model, the "capacity model," and that relative unit costs for in-house use, circulation, and reference are in the ratio of 1:1:2.6.

Cost and service data from 65 science and technology libraries of all sizes and with budgets ranging from $20,000 a year to $2,000,000 were studied and found to fit the above model. The author makes six broad conclusions about the study:

1. It is possible for a great range of libraries to collect and quantify data relating to in-house activities;
2. Models can be created which account for 70 percent of the variance in total costs of operation, models which describe

cost as a function only of *service rendered*, and not of intermediate variables such as staff, volumes added, etc.;
3. Deviation from the models does not depend on library size or library type;
4. The best-fit models show economy of scale;
5. Data on 2,000 reference questions provides the beginnings of a data set for defining norms and standards for the availability of reference service;
6. There is a growing interest in quantifying the relations between costs and output, and that such relations may be thought of as "economic laws for the operation of scientific and technical libraries."

As Kantor points out in his introduction, "without measure and documentation the library is at the mercy of institutional good will—a quality which vanishes quite as fast as the supply of disposable funds."

## TAXONOMY AND SCIENCE LIBRARIES

Biological nomenclature and classification applied to information retrieval. *Aslib Proceedings*. 33(4): 121–192; 1981 April.

This issue of the *Proceedings* is devoted to reports of papers presented at a meeting of the Aslib Biological and Agricultural Sciences Group held in London in 1980. Various approaches to the problem of access to biological literature were presented. The papers included discussions of taxonomic systems for the plant kingdom, cultivated plants, bacteria, zoological nomenclature, viruses, and animal health and hygiene. Papers were also read on the CAB database (Commonwealth Agricultural Bureau), MeSH, the UDC, the Barnard classification scheme for medical and veterinary libraries, and the system devised by A. Sandison for the British Library Science Reference Library collection.

## JOURNAL COST STUDY

McDonough, Carol C. *A simultaneous equation model of the demand for academic and professional journals*. Lowell, MA: Lowell University; 1982; April; PB 82-214248; PC A11/MF A01. 250 pp.

The author reports on an NSF grant to develop a simultaneous equation model for journal demand, which is defined as journal circulation levels or number of subscribers. The advantage of simultaneous equations is that they allow for possible interrelationships among journal demand, price and journal quality, and that regression analysis can be used to explain causal relationships such as that of price on demand. As the author theorized: "in the journals industry, journals with greater demand will have lower average costs, and thus will be able to charge lower prices. Likewise, journal demand is typically assumed to depend on journal quality; with higher quality journals experiencing greater demand."

The author's study, which was conducted on thirty-four economics journals published from 1974 to 1979 documented that commercial publishers charge the highest prices, followed by associations, and then universities, and that commercial journals tend to increase their prices more rapidly. The conclusion is reached that journal prices are not determined solely on the basis of average cost, and that "in fact, lower cost journals tend to have higher prices." There seems to be a tendency among the journals studied for journal publishers to set price, at least to some extent, according to "whatever the market will bear."

The same methodology should be applicable to other disciplines that index both their scientists and their journal articles by field of specialization.

## ARE COMPUTERS WORTH IT?

Kalus, C. *Network structured database design for the management of serials*. Oxford, England: Oxford University, Radcliffe Science Library; 1978 October; PB 82-145715. 27p.

Shaw, D. *An investigation of the costs and benefits of on-line serials handling*. Oxford, England: Oxford University, Radcliffe Science Library; 1980 Dec.; PB 82-803008. 15p.

The Radcliffe Science Library of Oxford University has a serials file of about 10,000 titles in approximately fifty specialized department libraries. A study was undertaken to determine whether the ordering, checking in, claiming, cataloging, binding and fiscal management of the collection could be cost-effective. The analysis was to cover five stages: systems analysis of the existing manual operations; an analysis of the costs of the manual system; the design and implementation of an online system; the enumeration of the benefits and faults of the automated system; and an evaluation of the costs and an assessment of the performance of the system.